Terrence M. Moore
Principal
Rise Up Academy

D1059073

I am thrilled to see this book come to print. Everywhere I do Circle training with people working with youth, I see a need for this book. The deeply moving work with youth at Roca and Carolyn's profound capacity for observation and reflection offer inspiration, wisdom, and hope that as a society we can do better for our young people than we have been doing. In the process of making space for healing our youth, we will heal ourselves.

—Kay Pranis

Peacemaking Circle Trainer and Facilitator; Coauthor of Peacemaking Circles: From Crime to Community *and Author of* The Little Book of Circle Processes

Young people naturally want to make people feel better. Circles provide a model by which they can do that collectively without judgment and in their own space. Youth who are living in challenging situations and dealing with multiple barriers feel a sense of empowerment in the sacred space of the Circle. It is probably the only place in the world where they make up their own rules and challenge each other to live by them. The depth of relationship created in Circle surpasses any other relationship anywhere.

Young people are constantly challenged to live a certain way, but they often have no model by which to do that. We as adults say to them, "Do as I say, not as I do." Circles provide a place and model for being the best human being you can be. All the youth at Roca who engaged in the Circle process felt a sense of empowerment and responsibility to their community.

—Gwen Chandler-Rhivers

Restorative Justice Processes Trainer and Author of the forthcoming LJP book, Creating Space at the Table: Being Intentional about Antiracism in Restorative Justice

For more comments about this book as well as about the growing use of Circles with young people, see page 259.

PEACEMAKING CIRCLES & URBAN YOUTH:

Bringing Justice Home

Carolyn Boyes-Watson

FOREWORD

The Reverend Dr. Martin Brokenleg

Living Justice Press
ST. PAUL, MINNESOTA

Living Justice Press
St. Paul, Minnesota 55105

*For information about permission to reproduce selections from this book,
please contact:*
Permissions, Living Justice Press, 2093 Juliet Avenue, St. Paul, MN 55105
Tel. (651) 695-1008 or contact permissions through our
Web site: www.livingjusticepress.org.

Library of Congress Cataloging-in-Publication Data

Boyes-Watson, Carolyn.
    Peacemaking circles and urban youth : bringing justice home /
Carolyn Boyes-Watson ; foreword, Martin Brokenleg. — 1st ed.
        p.   cm.
    Includes bibliographical references and index.
    ISBN 978-0-9721886-4-7 (alk. paper)
    1. Community-based corrections.   2. Restorative justice.   3. Healing
circles.   4. Urban youth—United States—Social conditions.   5. Identity
(Psychology) in youth—United States.   6. Problem youth—United States—
Rehabilitation.   7. Youth and violence—United States.   I. Title.
    HV9279.B69   2008
    364.6'8—dc22

                                                        2008012490

12 11 10 09 08   5 4 3 2
Copyediting by Cathy Broberg
Cover design by David Spohn
Interior design by Wendy Holdman
Printed by Sheridan Books, Ann Arbor, Michigan
on Nature's Book recycled paper

All photos courtesy of Roca, Inc.
The cover photo is of members of *Essencia Latina*, a professional dance company
based at Roca, whose main goals are to enhance cultural awareness in their community, improve young people's self-esteem, perform in many different dance
competitions, and, above all, help the dancers replace feelings of hopelessness
with empowerment and opportunity.

Contents

Foreword

Let us put our minds together and see what kind of
life we can make for our children.

SITTING BULL

Years ago Paula Gunn Allen, then a Native American professor of
English in California, said, "The longer White people live here, the
more Indian they will become." Dr. Allen's point was to acknowledge the deep effect of the land on any people who live in North
America. For Native people, the earth is not an abstract or inani-
mate commodity that we live on. She is the nurturing caregiver
that sustains our life and the lives of all beings on this planet.
When we Lakota people speak of the earth as our mother, we are
not being romantic poets. We are expressing a fundamental difference between our experience and that of Eurocentric cultures.
Our experience is that the earth is alive and she influences us in
all respects, particularly in how we live.

Carolyn Boyes-Watson's work is within the influence of
mother earth. For some time, Living Justice Press has shown
its serious inclusion of Native voices in its work. The Press has
published materials that make use of First Nations' ways of interacting, most notably in the use of talking Circles. *Peacemaking
Circles and Urban Youth* details the use of Native American ways
of relating with a population not necessarily familiar with Native
ways. Creating respectful, responsible youth cannot be based on
what we have done in the past, but it can emerge from new ways
of relating to youth. Talking Circles can provide urban youth at

risk—youth of any ethnic background—an experience of becoming responsible.

Talking Circles demonstrate an egalitarian interaction that gives each person in the Circle a place equal to that of others in the Circle. Even the physical arrangement of a Circle shows the equality of the participants. The dynamic of pace allows for full respect and meditative interaction in searching one's own mind and feelings. Solitary turns to speak allow each person to be listened to and heard. Youth of any status are not likely to be treated with respect in North America. The legacy of youth as property and commodity has existed since the time of Charles Dickens. The talking Circle format advocated as peacemaking Circles provide a new environment for youth of any ancestry to be understood and treated with the innate dignity that is their birthright.

The wisdom of Native Americans emerges from highly developed notions of relationship and preservation of functioning relationships under all circumstances. Guarding relationships directs how Native people relate to the physical earth. Preserving relationships should be the primary directive in assisting all youth to find their authentic voice and mature to the positive contributors to society they are by design.

Carolyn Boyes-Watson brings the wisdom of the Circle as the medicine for youth at risk. She documents the Circle as a philosophy, an ecological method of relating, and a healing intervention with youth, bringing them to responsibility. In our time, we know clearly that punishment only makes youth obedient. To transform youth into responsible youth and young adults requires the alchemy of respectful discipline. The writing of Carolyn Boyes-Watson uses the wisdom of the Circle to construct peace in the hearts of youth. Such youth do not need rules and laws to guide them from the outside. A mature heart guides them from their center. Confidant, courageous youth will result from using the ideas gathered and expressed by Carolyn Boyes-Watson.

—*The Reverend Dr. Martin Brokenleg*
Vice President, Reclaiming Youth International

Dedication

Vichey Phoung

This book is dedicated to Vichey Phoung, an amazing young man who taught all of us so very much about what it means to live. Vichey Phoung was born in a Thai refugee camp while his family was fleeing from the Cambodian Killing Fields. He came to the United States as a baby. In early adolescence, he joined a gang with his three older brothers and spent many years in and out of the streets. Over time and after a particularly challenging several months in jail, Vichey came to accept responsibility for causing harm and made remarkable and long-lasting changes in his life.

At Roca, he worked and volunteered as a streetworker. He sought out his peers and helped young people leave gangs. He kept peacemaking Circles for gang peace efforts, helped launch the VIA Project [Vision, Intent, and Action], and became a well-known young leader in the area. At age twenty-three, Vichey was tragically killed in an industrial accident. Vichey's surviving relatives include his mother, brothers, and son, Allen. In spite of his young age, Vichey had become in his own right a wise young person, whom we all loved and admired. To this day, Vichey's impact on Roca can be felt strongly. This dedication is from all of us at Roca who love him and miss him.

Acknowledgments

I am indebted to the all the people at Roca who sat with me and generously and candidly shared their thoughts and experiences of Circle. I have very fond memories of those sessions. Molly Baldwin welcomed me to Roca and afforded me the awesome chance to participate in the organization's extraordinary journey to learn Circle, an experience that gifted me with lifelong friendships as well as life-changing lessons. Roca's mentors are also my teachers: I want to thank Barry Stuart, Harold Gatensby, Mark Wedge, Gwen Chandler-Rivers, Don Johnson, and, especially, Kay Pranis, for the wisdom you have shared. It has truly been an inspiration to walk beside you.

This book would not exist without the vision, intelligence, and boundless energy of the dedicated staff and board of Living Justice Press. Living Justice Press is a testament to their abiding passion and commitment to creating profound and lasting change in the world. Kay Pranis deserves special credit for insisting that this book be written and for finding a way to make that happen. Denise Breton has been the perfect editor: masterful, committed, and brilliant in supporting the ideas and spirit of the book.

A final thanks goes to my precious family: Mark, Emily, and Matthew. You are my rock.

Gratitude from Living Justice Press

This book has had a long journey into print. It has been on our list to publish for five years. Part of this journey involved the process of documenting Roca's ongoing development in exploring the transformative potential of Circles at all levels of their organization and work. From the publishing side, the journey has involved the challenge to generate the necessary funding. For several years, we faced an impasse, as foundations consistently declined to fund book publishing, favoring instead direct service projects. So the manuscript sat, and at times we all despaired of its ever coming to print.

Then in 2007, a family chose to embark on what became an extraordinary journey of transformation. After years of animosity and estrangement, this family sought the help of Kay Pranis as Circle keeper and showed great courage and commitment as they engaged the Circle process. Together they explored the kind of challenging and sometimes painful issues that many families carry within their lives and histories together. During more than forty-five hours of intense and committed Circle work, family members learned once again to trust one another and came to embrace the Circle process and its values. Today, without Kay's assistance, they continue to mend their relationships.

Kay, who had long hoped to find the financial support to publish this book, proposed that, instead of compensating her for her time, the family might consider making a donation toward the funds necessary to produce this book—an amount over three times what

Kay's fee would have been. Family members agreed and, amazingly, the entire amount was donated. It is a gift beyond what we could imagine, and it means the book has come into existence in every way as a result of the Circle process. Not only the words in these pages but also the means to pay for copyediting, typesetting, and printing them came from a love of the Circle and an appreciation of how it can bring us together "in a good way."

Realizing that we cannot depend on foundations for support, we have reached out to individuals. Those of you who regularly buy and use our books keep us going, both financially and in spirit. In addition, we are deeply grateful to those of you who have chosen to support us on an ongoing basis—some as volunteers, some as donors, some as both. Because publishing is so expensive, and because we try to keep the price of books as low as we can (some books on restorative justice cost as much as $50, $100, or even $150), we could not possibly make these books available without your help.

So, our deep and abiding gratitude goes to Lisa Albrecht, Sherry Behm, Margaret Berrisford, Andrea Bosbach, Gerald Breidel, Ernie Breton, Jeannine Breton, Mary Joy Breton, Joan Breves, Cathy Broberg, Loretta Draths, Clark Erickson, Sid Farrar, Deb Feeny, Bridget Fensholt, Barbara Gerten, Rita A. Guild, Sister Teresa A. Hadro, Don Haldeman, Fred Hanauer, Jake Hanauer, Wendy Holdman, Karin E. Holser, Don Johnson, Wanda K. Joseph, Christopher Largent, Harriette Manis, Ann Mathews-Lingen, Maria Mazzara, Bob Moran, Ruth Newman, Marjorie Noonsong, Melanie Ounsworth, Kay Pranis, Susan Sharpe, Pat Siljenberg, Roger E. Sonnesyn, David Spohn, Sue Stacey, Yako Tahnaga, Joan Thalhuber, Margaret Thalhuber, Pat Thalhuber, Howard Vogel, Jill Warren, to one anonymous donor, and to the family of Miriam, Malcolm, Kurt, Kristin, Laurel, and Eric Lein. *Thank you!*

—Denise Breton, executive director, on behalf of
the board and staff of Living Justice Press

The Voices in this Book

Forty-three people were interviewed—several more than once—over the span of several years to gather the stories and insights for this book. The first wave of intensive, three- to four-hour interviews were conducted at the end of the second year of using peacemaking Circles. At that time, Roca asked me to conduct an evaluation of the lessons that they were learning from the Circles. So I talked at length with the young staff and the community partners who had been intensely involved in learning about Circles and implementing them. Most young staff members were in their late teens or early twenties and almost all had "grown up" at Roca, having been drawn there when they were gang-involved, immigrant, or street-wise teens.

These taped interviews constitute the bulk of the story shared here. About a year later, Roca asked me to interview people outside the organization, such as city officials, police, social workers, teachers, clergy, and administrators who had participated in the Circles at Roca and who, in some instances, had begun to use them for themselves within their own organizations.

The voices from all these interviews form the trunk of this book, which has been leafed out by my own observations and explanations. During these years, I have participated in countless Circles, events, trainings, and meetings at Roca, and as a result, I have witnessed many stories and experiences. These have also found their way into the voices woven throughout the text.

After much consideration, I have chosen to identify staff at

Roca by their first names but to keep the identities of those who work outside of Roca anonymous. These interviewees are described by their job position and title. This approach provides a screen for those who prefer anonymity, yet it allows the strength of the voices to shine through. In the stories about specific young people at Roca, the names are fictional to protect their privacy.

—*Carolyn Boyes-Watson*
February 2008

PEACEMAKING CIRCLES & URBAN YOUTH

CHAPTER ONE

The Gift of Circles

This book is about the use of peacemaking Circles as a strategy to build positive connections among marginalized youth and families in inner cities. In a larger sense, this book is also about justice. How can we live in a good way with each other? This is the ultimate question of justice. If we want to build good relations with each other or redress the genuine roots of conflicts and harms, thinking about justice in terms of detentions, courts, and prisons fails to help us. Punishment seldom strengthens good relations. In truth, it often takes a difficult situation and makes things worse.

"How can we live in a good way with each other?" is what peacemaking Circles are all about. The peacemaking Circle is an ancient social practice embedded within Indigenous and non-Western societies. It is a way of bringing people together to talk from our deepest values and our best selves. By helping us build relationships and strengthen communities, Circles invite a way of being together that feels like what we all want and hope justice could be.

The justice that grows from Circles is not something we can easily put into words. Circles help us come together in a good way not only when it is easy but especially when it is hard. Sometimes it is when people come to a Circle with the most pain and sense of division that they leave with the deepest sense of having experienced justice. They have experienced the justice of being heard, the justice of being respected, the justice of hearing others speak from their hearts, and the justice of working things out in ways that honor the needs of everyone involved.

For young people, this experience of justice is often lacking from their lives. Youth often do not feel heard or respected. They do not feel their views or needs count. How they see and experience their lives does not seem to be honored. This can be true for all youth, even youth of privilege. But for marginalized youth, most of whom are youth of color, the experience of injustice in everyday relationships can be overwhelming. It is no wonder, then, that the growing use of Circles with youth is transforming not only young people but also those who share their lives.

Seven years ago, Roca, a feisty community-based youth organization that serves one of the most broken and dangerous urban neighborhoods near Boston, adopted peacemaking Circles in its work with youth and young adults. This is the story of Roca's journey to practice the obvious—and not so obvious—lessons of the Circle.

My purpose in writing this book is to share Roca's experience, so that others may learn about the peacemaking Circle's potential and power. The dominant paradigms for addressing social problems in this culture come from our experiences of making war. We declare war on poverty, crime, illness, and drug addiction. Justice itself is often conceived as a battleground in which forces of good triumph by destroying forces of evil. Within our legal system, each side comes armed with the resources to outmaneuver the other. The defeated side is forced to submit to state punishment—a systematic imposition of violence that is intended to restore balance through the harm inflicted on the guilty party.

Today we are waging war on our youth, and most concertedly, on poor youth of color. Policies of zero tolerance and a youth justice system modeled after the adult punitive system attack young people, as if they are the cause of the problem rather than the bearers of its most disturbing symptoms. As a result, we do not respond to troubled behavior with connection, support, listening, responsiveness, caring, compassion, or love. Instead, we increasingly rely on surveillance, detention, suspension, expulsion, and incarceration. In the name of discipline, security, or safety, we intentionally destroy young people's futures.

Roca is committed to a positive vision of young people in the world. In their words, "Roca's mission is to promote justice through creating opportunities for young people to become self-sufficient and to live out of harm's way." The peacemaking Circle is one among several strategies they have adopted to try to create a world where all young people are valued and cared for. If the essence of a war-based model is destruction, the essence of peacemaking Circles is creation. Whether it is in the family, schools, peer groups, social services, or courts, the peacemaking Circle opens possibilities for figuring out together how to create better, more just relationships within society. Peace is not simply the absence of war but the presence of justice. In the final analysis, if we want peace, we have to practice justice.

The book starts by giving the reader a picture of the challenges facing the urban youth who come to Roca. The young people who pass through Roca's doors carry the burden of tremendous injustices in their lives, few of which will ever be acknowledged, much less remedied, by our formal legal institutions. Chapter 2 describes the "modern monsters" that permeate the landscape in which many youth live. Neglect, discrimination, racism, violence, poverty, abuse, addiction, incarceration, despair, rage, and hopelessness: these form the backdrop for their growth and development as young men and women. To understand fully why young people behave as they sometimes do, we need to understand the contexts shaping their behavior.

In contrast to these modern monsters, chapter 3 describes the model of positive youth development at Roca. It explains the overall set of strategies that Roca uses as a youth and community development organization, and then it shows how peacemaking Circles fit in with Roca's larger mission.

The next four chapters analyze four distinct avenues through which peacemaking Circles make a difference in the lives of young people and their communities. The first and often most visible impact of Circles is how they open young people's voices. Chapter 4 examines how peacemaking Circles create opportunities for the talents, ideas, wisdom, and energies of all members of the community—including those most silenced and most marginalized—to be genuinely seen and heard.

Chapter 5 investigates how Circles create a space for holding oneself and others accountable for behaving with integrity in the world. Accountability is a core principle of justice. Practicing accountability has to do with learning how to rectify the poor choices we sometimes make in our conduct toward others and ourselves. In this chapter, we examine how peacemaking Circles support young people in modeling and practicing personal and collective responsibility. In very concrete ways, they learn how to practice justice—how to "put things right."

Chapter 6 explores the power of Circles to promote emotional awareness and healing. Those participating in Circles experience a deep sense of safety. This safety enables people to express the difficult and often suppressed emotions that are a source of so much destruction and violence in relationships. In the unique space that Circles create, participants develop the trust they need to voice their vulnerabilities. As they explore tender and often submerged emotions, they gain more control over their behavior and choices. Moreover, by honoring the harms people suffer, the Circle restores to the community its power of compassionate witnessing. Witnessing harms with compassion helps a community overcome violence. Circle participants can express moral solidarity with those who have been harmed as well as address the underlying reasons for the harmful behavior.

Chapter 7 widens the focus beyond the youth organization to examine how Circles affect the formal systems that have been exposed to the Circle process through their partnerships with Roca.

Without systemic change within major social institutions, genuine transformation is hard to imagine, much less hope for. In the seven years of practicing Circles at Roca, many outsiders to Roca have been exposed to the practice and have begun to use Circles within their own organizations. This chapter explores the impact of Circles on adults who work with marginalized youth and their families across the state of Massachusetts, primarily within the state's Department of Social Services (DSS) and the Department of Youth Services (DYS).

The final chapter, "Bringing Justice Home," returns to the theme of justice by asking: Can Circles offer a path toward creating a more just society? The injustices within our society rarely find remedy within the narrow confines of our legal system. Indeed, the young people at Roca are quite cynical about the meaning of justice within our society. They are not cynical, however, about peacemaking Circles. Quite the opposite, they intuit a deep connection between their experiences within Circles and a very different meaning of justice that emerges for themselves and their communities as a result.

My Voice in This Book

As a sociologist employed by an urban university, I have spent many years teaching about the self-perpetuating failure of the criminal justice system and the absence of justice for victims, offenders, and communities. Inside the classroom, my students and I have examined the legacy of past injustices and the ongoing violence of profound structural and social inequalities. Yet, for many years, I had little to offer students as a more satisfying alternative. This changed when I discovered the modern restorative justice movement.

"Restorative justice" is a broad and often controversial term. It generally refers to a growing social movement to practice peaceful, constructive approaches to violations of legal and human rights. To this end, restorative justice also promotes deeper levels of problem-solving in human relations. These restorative approaches range from international peacemaking tribunals, such as the Truth and Reconciliation Commission in South Africa, to innovations within our criminal justice system, schools, social services, and communities.

In my view, the restorative justice paradigm widens our lens beyond the current legal system and reconnects us with a deeper sense of justice that resides within our own human experiences. Justice is an essential element to living well with other human beings. To create communities that thrive, we must live in a way that satisfies an abiding need we all have for just social institutions. Much of the sustained violence in the world arises from social arrangements that violate this basic human need. Indeed, the growing environmental crises suggest that issues of justice extend to our relations with the natural world as well.

As a reform movement within the dominant society, restorative justice started within the criminal justice system. Over several decades, it has served to guide positive, step-by-step changes in our courts, correctional systems, and policing. The peacemaking Circle process is one of several practices now being used as an alternative to traditional sentencing and other criminal justice mechanisms for responding to violations and harms.

But the wisdom inherent in the peacemaking Circle process as well as in restorative justice principles can help us learn to live justly far beyond the narrow scope of criminal law. As those involved with Roca have discovered, walking the talk of peacemaking Circles is about learning to live in a better relationship with oneself and others. It is about learning to "be in a good way"—to develop respectful, mutually supportive relationships—within families, organizations, communities, and governments. Ultimately, Circles are about justice and the profoundly hopeful possibility that we can—together—create better, more just ways to live with each other. At the end of the day, sitting in Circle is about learning a different "way to be" in the world.

In writing this book, I did not set out to design a research project that isolates the effects of the peacemaking Circle on a specific set of behaviors or outcomes. While social scientific research that measures specific outcomes is extremely important, that is not what this book is. Some might find that I am more of a social observer than a sociologist in these pages.

Yet I am not a neutral observer in writing this book. I believe in the potential of the peacemaking Circle to make a difference in people's lives, and I set out to describe both what others have experienced and what I myself have witnessed.

It is true that some who approached the Circle did so with skepticism, sarcasm, distrust, and animosity. Some people—both within Roca and outside it—were wary of Circles and objected to them as boring, inefficient, or silly. In some cases, these people simply refused to participate. Although I don't provide much detail about the (surprisingly infrequent) occasions when peacemaking Circles devolved into shouting matches or when people refused to participate by not showing up or not honoring the talking piece, I nonetheless think it is important for readers to realize that this sometimes happened. To imagine that Circles were universally accepted would be fairyland fiction.

I am not interested, however, in the resistance that Roca experienced in bringing peacemaking Circles to people unfamiliar with its unique format. To me, it is far more important to investigate why so many people *are* drawn to Circles. Why does the Circle process affect people so profoundly? Specifically, I wanted to dissect the Circle's power. What is sociologically distinct about the Circle process from so many other ways that we come together to talk with one another?

I wanted to consider, for example:

- What makes a Circle different from a meeting?
- Why do people feel a powerful sense of connection with others, even those they barely know, after they have sat together in Circle?
- Why are some young people, who otherwise may be completely silent in the company of adults, willing to open up inside Circles that include adults?
- What makes young people, who are notoriously un-willing or unable to focus on a teacher in the class-room, able to sit—sometimes for hours—simply listening?
- What do Circles bring that is otherwise missing from our lives and relationships?
- And, finally, what is the purpose of learning to practice this Indigenous ritual within a multiethnic inner-city neighborhood that is struggling with issues of poverty, marginalization, racism, violence, crime, abuse, and institutional, systemic oppression?

In essence, this book is a case study about Circles that intensely and closely describes the experiences of one organization in one place and at one particular time. In the chapters of this book, I tease apart the different aspects of the Circle and all the ways that sitting in Circle has affected the lives of young people. I talk, for example, about the power of the Circle to help young people practice emotional literacy and heal emotional wounds; its ability to open spaces for youth empowerment, inspiration, and voice; and its practical power in teaching habits of respect, responsibil-ity, and accountability. I also examine the impact of the Circle on grown-ups within our society, both in how adults interact with youth and in how adults occupy positions of power within our society.

My hope is that this story will speak to readers who are in many different places. The Roca of today still practices peacemaking Circles, even while the organization has continued to evolve and change. I describe in fair detail how peacemaking Circles fit into the overall strategies and programs of this particular organization. My purpose is to show readers how peacemaking Circles can become part of the normal routines and rhythms of our own everyday settings, whether they be school, workplace, family, or community.

The Gifting of Peacemaking Circles

How did Roca come to learn about the peacemaking Circle? It began in 1999. One of the early ventures of the Center for Restorative Justice at Suffolk University, located in Boston, Massachusetts, was to host a conference on restorative justice. The conference showcased restorative justice principles—and the Circle sentencing process, in particular—as a community-based alternative to the adversarial, punitive court model. The speakers included Judge Barry Stuart, former Chief Justice of the Yukon Territorial Courts; Howard Zehr, known as the grandfather of the modern restorative justice movement; and Kay Pranis, who at that time was the Restorative Justice Planner for Minnesota's Department of Corrections. Molly Baldwin, the executive director of Roca, attended the conference, accompanied by a number of Roca's young staff. The Roca attendees were instantly enthralled with the potential of the peacemaking Circle process for positive youth development. They relentlessly pursued the presenters during the conference, until they agreed to come back and teach them how to practice the Circle.

Within three months, Barry Stuart returned to Boston, bringing with him Don Johnson, an assistant county attorney from Minnesota, and Mark Wedge, Aan Goosh Oo of the Deicitaan Clan of the Tagish/T'lingit Nation. Mark had been instrumental in teaching Barry and Don about Circles and how to adapt them to the Western judicial system. For many years, Mark had worked with Aboriginal and Western systems to incorporate traditional teachings into contemporary processes in order to bring diverse people together. His aim was to protect and promote Indigenous rights and interests. Harold Gatensby, House Leader of the Kookchittaan Clan, Kay Pranis, and African American community activist Gwen Chandler-Rhivers later joined Roca's Circle-coaching team of Barry, Don, and Mark.

Over the next two years, these six mentors would return to Roca many times, and staff from Roca would visit, call, or email them for guidance. They conducted numerous four-day trainings for Roca and its expanding community, which eventually included not only staff and youth but also parents, teachers, social workers, city and state employees, administrators, and criminal justice personnel. Through this period of intense learning, the Circle-mentoring team counseled, taught, coached, did troubleshooting, supported, and encouraged the Roca community in its growing use of Circles at every level of its operations.

The peacemaking Circle was thus given to Roca and other Westerners by Indigenous individuals who were willing not only to share the wisdom of their ancestors but also to do so with a culture that has all but destroyed this precious heritage. Indigenous Peoples have struggled to relearn and reestablish principles and practices that have been violently repressed through the genocidal policies of Western governments over centuries. After all the effort to preserve and protect Native knowledge for Native people, why would these Indigenous individuals expend their energies to share their cultural peacemaking practices with non-Native communities? Why invite the inevitable dilution and cooptation by the dominant Anglo culture?

The gift of peacemaking Circles represents an extraordinary act of generosity and expression of solidarity with non-Native Peoples. Perhaps they gave this gift in the hope that non-Native

Peoples would learn a way of being in relationship that is different from the institutionally arrogant, hierarchical, and controlling patterns that have brought such suffering to Native Peoples. Perhaps they hoped Circles could help us learn how to be "good relatives" to each other. Certainly the gift of Circles reflects the deep wisdom that we are all in this together. Unless we humans learn to change our ways together, we have little hope of saving the rivers, mountains, plants, animals, and oceans of this earth—not to mention ourselves.

A gift is an act of faith. It expresses an inherent willingness to let go, since a gift, once given, no longer belongs to the giver. The peacemaking Circle process was given to Roca, and from there, it has been offered to each and every person who sits in a Circle and is open to its ways. Invariably and inevitably, the Circle is reformed to fit the rhythms, traditions, and cultures of new users. Like a story that passes from mouth to ear, the ritual of the peacemaking Circle changes each time it is learned anew. The spirit of the gift brings a generous freedom that allows the recipient to reshape the gift, so that it becomes truly useful in one's own home.

On the receiver's side, a gift brings obligations. One obligation is to honor the origins of the gift—to remember where it came from. With the gift of the Circle comes the obligation to hold in view the sacred intention of those who shared it with such largess. Seven years down the road, Roca remains explicitly grateful to the Tagish/T'lingit People and to the six teachers who opened doors to so much growth and development. With gratitude has come a deep desire to honor these teachers by recognizing the gift and acknowledging it as such, even as Roca transforms the Circle to become an ongoing part of its own community.

This gift also comes with an enduring challenge—to learn the deeper wisdom of the peacemaking Circle and to honor that wisdom by doing one's best to walk in its ways. A gift reflects commitments of the heart, and the Circle teaches a great deal about opening pathways to the heart. To accept the gift of the peace-making Circle, then, is to accept the challenge to walk the ways of peace with oneself, loved ones, struggling ones, strangers, the larger community, and the world. With the gift of Circles comes a growing awareness that, despite all of our profound differences, we are also—as human beings—one and the same.

CHAPTER TWO

Urban Youth and Modern Monsters

"Young people got so much to say, but they've been neglected for so many years—just left out on the street. They want to talk to people, and they want to share this stuff and their pain, and yet they don't know how to do it in a good way."

VICHEY, ROCA STAFF

A Place Where Everyone Belongs

In 1988 Molly Baldwin was twenty-something and had a passion for young people. "I was a community organizer, so the first thing we did together was community organizing. I guess if I was a basketball player, we would have played basketball." Roca began its organizational life as a teen pregnancy prevention program. Its first grant funded an initiative to take pregnant teens rowing on the Charles River. "It didn't really matter what we were doing together: what mattered was the connection."

The name *Roca* means *rock* in Spanish. According to Molly, "Roca creates a place that is like a rock, a solid foundation. It is a place of power, and it is about the strength of youth, families, and our communities." The founding vision of Roca was to create a place where all young people could belong. More than anything, young people need a genuine connection with adults who believe in them and who will stand by them as they face the challenges of growing up. It doesn't matter which particular activity brings adults and young people together: what matters is the relationship and that it acts as a positive force in a young person's life.

For its first eight years, the physical space of Roca was no more than a pair of storefronts, first in downtown Chelsea and later in Revere on Shirley Avenue. These modest spaces served as offices and a home base for a dozen or so youth workers who fanned out into the street corners, schoolyards, abandoned lots, courthouses, and front porches of the community, always seeking to build relationships with disconnected teens. As relationships blossomed, young people gravitated to the tiny storefronts, overfilling the cramped spaces and spilling onto the corner and sidewalks of the city.

Today Roca occupies a two-story building in the heart of downtown Chelsea. The handsome, whitewashed building sits elegantly among the red brick buildings of the city square. A former automobile showroom, the building houses a recreation center, a health clinic, a dance studio, a basketball court, a daycare center, computer labs, and classrooms. Now a $6.1 million enterprise, Roca works in-

Roca's building at 101 Park Street, Chelsea, Massachusetts

tensively with over six hundred youth and young people each year. It also provides less intensive services to 350-plus young people and parents, and it affects an additional twenty thousand through community outreach. Forty-seven full-time adult staff, seventeen part-time staff, and forty part-time and/or transitional employment youth staff provide transformational relationships, life skills, education, and employment services.

Huge windows covered in painted murals and hand-painted flyers welcome people to the activities taking place inside. The doorway is nearly always framed by clusters of young people, staff, and visitors on their way in or out of the building and is especially crowded after 3:00 p.m. and on weekend nights. Cars honk and people wave as they greet one another at the busy intersection where one of Roca's eight vans are often stopped, unloading groceries, dropping young people off from school, or taking them to a game of soccer.

The Urban Villages of Roca

Sayra, a fourteen-year-old Indian immigrant from Honduras, had a vision of a place she needed in her life. Like many others, Sayra "grew up" at Roca. She found there the relationships she needed to thrive and lead change for herself and her community. Now a thirty-year-old graduate of Middlebury College, Sayra explains her vision of Roca: "If we want community to move from a place of isolated ethnic enclaves who are not really participating in this society to a place where communities decide how resources get spent, where buildings get built, and so forth, then the question is how to access and harness that creative power, so people can actualize their vision for themselves and their children for seven generations to come."

Roca works with young people from the communities of Chelsea, Revere, Lynn, Charlestown, and East Boston—neighboring communities with similar socioeconomic conditions. Chelsea lies on the northern edge of Boston with an official population of just under 40,000. Hidden in the shadow of highways and bridges that serve as major arteries for the metropolitan area, Chelsea covers a dense 1.8 square miles of urban landscape. Flanked by the Mystic River and Boston Harbor, the streets are lined with multi-family triple-deckers and single-family houses, reflecting the city's long history as home to first-generation immigrants. Today, Latino immigrants from Central and South America as well as from Puerto Rico, Mexico, and Cuba make up nearly half of the city's population.

Chelsea is among the poorest cities in Massachusetts. It has the lowest per capita income in the state—$14,628 a year.[1] Among its public school students, 77 percent are eligible for a free or reduced-price lunch, compared to a statewide average of 26 percent. Chelsea leads the state in the number of families headed by a single female (36.1 percent). According to official statistics, 23.2 percent of its population lives in poverty, and 18 percent of its households earn less than $10,000 a year. About 42 percent of Chelsea's youth live below the poverty level. The high school dropout rate in the city is over three times higher than the state average, and the unemployment rate (4.6 percent) is almost double the state average (2.5 percent). Although the teen birth rate has decreased by 30 percent within the last ten years, the rate for girls between the ages of fifteen and nineteen (80.8/1000) is more than three times the state average (24.3/1000).

North of Chelsea is the city of Revere. Geographically larger than Chelsea and more economically stable, Revere is a traditional White, working-class city with pockets of immigrant enclaves inhabiting blocks of treeless streets lined with multi-family housing. Once famous for its public beach, Revere is less dense than Chelsea. It has a higher per capita income ($19,463 a year), and fewer of its individuals live in poverty (14.5 percent). Half of the houses in Revere are owner-occupied, compared to 24 percent in Chelsea.

The city of Lynn lies north of Revere. Historically home to the textile mills of the nineteenth century, the city is eleven miles from Boston. Its industrial downtown is rich with the grandiose redbrick architecture of a bygone era. Covering eleven square miles, Lynn has a socioeconomic profile similar to Revere with a per capita income of $17,492 and with 16 percent of its individuals officially living in poverty. In Lynn public schools, almost half of the students are eligible for free or reduced-rate lunches.

Roca's work also extends to East Boston, a neighborhood adjacent to Chelsea and separated from the rest of the city by Boston Harbor. With a population that is nearly 40 percent Latino (the majority being foreign-born), East Boston closely resembles the demographics of Chelsea. The per capita income is slightly higher at $15,619 a year. Just under 20 percent of East Boston's residents live below the official poverty line, and 25 percent of the young people under the age of eighteen live in poverty. Among the adults in this neighborhood, 40 percent have neither a high school degree nor a GED equivalency. Compared to the city of Boston as a whole, the neighborhood of East Boston has very high rates of mortality from drug abuse: 25/100,000 versus 14/100,000 for the city as a whole.

The Peoples of the Urban Villages

"Wherever there is strife in the world, six months later we have people from that country living here in Chelsea, and the process of assimilation, it seems to me, seems to be getting tougher and tougher. Chelsea has always been an immigrant community, dating all the way back to the late 1800s and early 1900s with waves of immigrants. The difference between those days, when you had the Italians coming over and today, were all the different layers. You had a whole family and whole community that were looking after

each other. I don't get that sense anymore. . . . It's
a very competitive economy, and trades that once
existed and allowed people to earn a living wage and
support a family no longer exist, and the community
support no longer exists either."

CHELSEA CITY OFFICIAL

For over a century, all of these communities have served as gateways for immigrants to enter the United States. Chelsea and its near neighbors receive people from every corner of the world, including Central Asia (Pakistan, Afghanistan, Uzbekistan, Tajikistan); Eastern Europe (Albania, Bosnia); Africa (Morocco, Somalia, Sudan); the Caribbean (Haiti, Dominican Republic, Puerto Rico), Southeast Asia, (Cambodia, Vietnam, Thailand), and, most frequently in recent years, Central and South America (Honduras, El Salvador, Guatemala, Colombia, Peru, and Brazil). Based on data from 2002, of the 727 young people involved with Roca, 52 percent were Latino (both White and people of color); 25 percent Asian, generally Cambodian or Vietnamese; 11 percent African American or second-generation West Indies Black; and 10 percent White.

Just as Chelsea and its neighbors are multicultural, so, too, is life at Roca a blend of vividly different traditions and cultures. Roca cultural events include break-dancing, a Latin dance ensemble, a Bosnian dance group, an Albanian dance group, hip hop classes, Christian Sunday services, a women-only Muslim ESL (English as Second Language) class, a Bosnian movie night, a Sudanese young men's dinner, to name only a few of the cultural events. At the same time that the Muslim Al-Huda group holds women-only aerobic classes for Somali women, a salsa dance troupe practices their routine in another room. Sudanese young men meet for their weekly dinner, while Central American parents meet on education issues, and Cambodian elders and youth kneel in prayer on pillows in the gym. When Roca opens its doors to groups within the community to hold religious services in the building, the sounds of gospel mingle with the sweet smell of burning sage for the peacemaking Circles.

Chelsea itself has the highest percentage of foreign-born residents (36 percent) in the state, although official statistics do not reflect the true composition of the city. Both undocumented residents and those with documentation who fear the government and its census-takers are regularly undercounted. All the official statistics are distorted as a result, from the percentages of those who are foreign born to the numbers of those living in poverty, the unemployment rates, and the numbers of non-English-speaking residents. The official census counts 48.4 percent of Chelsea as Latino. Recent data from the Massachusetts Department of Education indicate that approximately 67 percent of Chelsea's schoolchildren are Latino, 17 percent are White, 9 percent are Black or African American, and 7 percent are Asian. As much as 79 percent of the children in Chelsea's public schools come from families where English is not the primary language spoken in the home. Twenty-two distinct languages are spoken within this densely packed 1.8 square miles, where the actual population is substantially higher than the 40,000 documented residents recorded by the U.S. census.

Many people living in these communities are refugees from war-torn countries. Revere and neighboring Lynn have the third largest population of Cambodians in the country, and most of them have experienced extreme deprivation, starvation, and violence as they fled the "killing fields" of the Cambodian holocaust. Of the estimated 171,000 Cambodians living in the United States, roughly 20,000 live in Massachusetts, and the greatest concentrations of Cambodians live in the cities of Lowell and Lynn. Far from the image of the "model minority," Asian Americans in Lynn remain apart from mainstream American life. According to the 2000 census data, 36 percent of the Asian Americans in the city over the age of twenty-five had less than a ninth-grade education, compared to 7 percent for both Whites and Blacks.

The neighborhood in Revere centering around Shirley Avenue was a thriving Jewish community until the late 1960s, when the affluent second generation abandoned the bustling urban village for the suburbs or the year-round warmth of Florida. Beginning in the 1980s, a steady stream of refugees from the camps of Southeast Asia began to settle on Shirley Avenue, changing store signs from Hebrew to Khymer. Between 1980 and 1995, more than 3,000 Cambodian refugees and their children relocated to the Shirley Avenue neighborhood. They were greeted with substantial racial discrimination and violence, including a firebombing on Christmas Eve that left two-dozen Cambodian residents homeless.

By 1991, gang violence erupted on Shirley Avenue as youth banded together to gain protection and to assert their own identity in the face of racial and ethnic assaults. The local police responded to the escalating violence with harassment and racial profiling. In the midst of the crisis, Roca opened its second storefront in Revere directly on Shirley Avenue to respond to the growing hostility within the community toward Cambodian youth.

Chelsea is also home to political refugees from Honduras, El Salvador, and Guatemala fleeing political persecution and civil war. Years of civil war in El Salvador, Guatemala, and Nicaragua spawned a massive exodus from the chaos, disorder, and political persecution in these countries. Millions fled north to the barrios of Los Angeles and to other poor urban enclaves, such as Chelsea or East Boston, leaving behind a social fabric destroyed by violence. Within recent years, a second generation of young immigrants raised in these decimated communities has begun to arrive through a complex network of gangs that reach across the north-south border.

At the age of fourteen, Edgar traveled from El Salvador, "illegal" and alone, in search of his older brother. Not understanding a word of English and without parents or other adults in his life, Edgar came north and successfully joined his brother. He was soon smoking marijuana, using heroin, and hanging

out with his brother and the local Salvadorean gang MS-13 on
the streets of Chelsea.

George, a streetworker from Roca, pays attention to this
group of Central American young men. A thirty-year-old
father of three, George was born in Puerto Rico, grew up in
Chelsea, and has been involved with Roca since his teens.
Every day, George—along with other streetworkers from
Roca—go out looking for chances to build connections and
relationships with young men and women ready for change.

Facing the Monsters of Modern Life

> "In the times of legend, Navajos slew monsters.
> Today, Navajos face new monsters . . . domestic
> violence, child abuse, and neglect . . . alcoholism. . . .
> These problems are today's monsters, . . . which get
> in the way of a successful life."
>
> ROBERT YAZZIE, CHIEF JUSTICE EMERITUS
> OF THE NAVAJO SUPREME COURT[2]

Young people in these communities confront considerable challenges as they seek a healthy path toward adulthood. The majority of Roca's young people experience disturbing—if not outright
traumatizing—situations in their lives. On top of normal adolescent turbulence, they routinely cope with violence, fear, abandonment, loss, neglect, economic hardship, discrimination, and
displacement. The adults in their lives are often unable to provide
the support they need, being traumatized, overwhelmed, struggling, absent, or incarcerated themselves. Alcoholism, drugs,
family violence, gangs, unemployment, rampant materialism,
sexual exploitation, cultural domination, and spiritual emptiness
are some of the powerful realities that plague the lives of Roca's
young people and challenge them every day. Chief Justice Yazzie
of the Navajo Supreme Court referred to these harsh realities as

the "monsters" of modern life. As with the mythic forces of evil, these dangers must be faced with courage and fortitude, if these young people are to make a successful journey to adulthood.

How do these "monsters" manifest themselves in the lives of Roca's youth? We can see their mayhem in reams of dreary statistics. In 2003, 14.6 percent of Chelsea high school students carried a weapon (such as a gun, knife, or club) within the past thirty days—a figure that was even higher (17.9 percent) among those in middle school.[3] Carrying weapons indicates the level of fear that the young people have for their personal safety. At least one day in the previous month, 11 percent of those in middle school and 8.3 percent of those in high school did not attend school because they felt unsafe, either at school or while traveling to and from school.

Living with this stress takes an emotional toll that can be seen in alarming statistics of attempted suicide: 9 percent of those in middle school and 12.7 percent of those in high school reported an attempted suicide at least once within the past twelve months. For some specific groups, this figure is even more heartbreaking: 19.7 percent of high school freshman reported an attempted suicide within the past twelve months.

The majority of young people at Roca have some interaction with social services, the courts, and the juvenile system. Depending on the age group, roughly one quarter to a third of the young people at Roca are on probation. Among the older, more street-involved participants, this figure is higher. At any given time, a significant percentage of the young people involved with Roca are incarcerated within either the juvenile or the adult system. Being incarcerated is one of the most significant factors that increase the odds of "negative outcomes" for youth as they transition to adulthood. For example, most juvenile offenders who are sixteen and older never return to formal education once they leave the juvenile justice system, and being locked up as a juvenile is one of the strongest predictors of adult incarceration.[4]

Two-thirds of the young people at Roca are between sixteen and thirty years old. A generation ago, people in this same age group would be on their own or closing in on that goal, holding down jobs that provided for their financial needs, and raising their own families. Today, stable adulthood no longer begins when adolescence ends. For most middle-class Americans, the late teens and twenties are a period of extended education, career development, and social maturation. And young people require significant financial and emotional support from their family of origin during this time.

Vulnerable young adults who lack this family support find it very difficult to take on these adult roles. Each year, approximately 20,000 eighteen-year-olds nationwide "age out" of foster care and find themselves without the support of kin that other youth can rely on.[5] On their own, these young people are less likely to be employed and more likely to be on public assistance than the general population. They are also more likely to remain single and to become involved with the criminal justice system.

Among those most at risk of being shut out of a successful adult future are young parents. Becoming pregnant remains the single most common reason that girls drop out of school, and only about

a third of teen mothers go on to get their high school diplomas after giving birth to a child.[6] Among young men who become teen fathers, less than half complete high school. Both young mothers and fathers are ill prepared to adequately raise and care for their children, both emotionally and materially.

Young girl at Roca

School failure is common among the young people at Roca. Some of the youth that Roca works with—those twelve and older—attend school but are at a high risk of dropping out. Many of the other youth and young adults at Roca have already dropped out of school or have been expelled. Most of the young people have poor attendance records and a history of negative experiences in the school environment.

At Chelsea High School, for example, more than a quarter of the freshman class is repeating the ninth grade for the second or third time. Fully 37 percent of Chelsea's public school population turns over each year, as poor families frequently move or children shuffle between foster homes and relatives. Some young adults at Roca, particularly new immigrants, have barely attended school at all, either in the United States or in their country of origin, and are illiterate in both English and their native tongue.

For immigrants and refugees, the challenges of living a healthy life are compounded by their status as illegal residents and by the cultural displacement they experience from living between two worlds. The children of these immigrants who were born in this country experience a double alienation: alienation from the world of their parents as well as from dominant, mainstream U.S. culture. Parents often do not learn English, nor are they aware of or sympathetic to the pressures that their children experience as members of U.S. culture. For both Latino and Cambodian youth, the norms and expectations of their parents for appropriate conduct, dress, speech, and deference to adults conflict with the dominant norms of American culture. This conflict further strains the relationship that youth have with their parents, as both struggle to adjust to a foreign culture.

Undocumented status and lack of English-speaking skills pose substantial barriers for immigrants to the United States. In Chelsea, newcomers (those who have arrived within the previous three years) constitute 30 percent of the officially counted population. Even more disconnected and fragile are the undocumented immigrants, who exist in unknown numbers on the extreme margins. A substantial proportion of these youth and young adults have been disconnected from stable families both in their countries of origin and in the United States. Most often, they immigrated to the United States to pursue an older cousin, sibling, or friend, and many have ties to gangs that reach from the barrios of Los Angeles or Chelsea to Honduras and Guatemala.

The burden of trauma magnifies the obstacles for immigrants who have fled war and violence. After the Cambodian holocaust in which millions perished, a substantial number of survivors immigrated with their children to the United States.[7] In recent years, newcomers from Bosnia, Afghanistan, Somalia, and Sudan have arrived in Chelsea in the wake of extreme chaos, violence, and disorder within their countries of origin. Parents and children who suffered the trauma of starvation, refugee camps, and war violence have high levels of post-traumatic stress and other psychological disorders.

Trauma is also elevated for those who were born here but raised in families with traumatized parents and siblings. Chronic depression, alcoholism, emotional dissociation, and dysfunction are common legacies of this exposure. So, too, is silence within the home and the community about the trauma and its aftermaths. This is especially true where cultural norms discourage open communication between parents and children. Moreover, the so-called 1.5 generation—young people born in Southeast Asia but raised here—face the increasing threat of being deported to a land that is as foreign to them as it is to any native-born American.

When he was three or four years old, Saroeum Phoung accompanied his father in the Cambodian army to the front lines to fight the Khmer Rouge. Years later, his father told him why he brought his young son with him to fight. "If I thought you would be killed, then I have anger to fight." Saroeum remembers seeing a bullet wound his father. As a small boy, he witnessed executions of many who tried to escape from the Khmer Rouge camp.

    When he was seven, Saroeum and his family escaped on foot over the mountains. Saroeum can still recall the image of his torn and bleeding feet as he begged his mother to leave him at the base of a tree. The family spent five years struggling in two refugee camps in Thailand before emigrating to the Unites States when Saroeum was twelve. Two years later, Saroeum moved to Chelsea. By then, he had formed a gang of Cambodian youth with similar refugee experiences.

The fact that so many young people at Roca are involved in gangs is not surprising. In communities weakened by the forces of war, poverty, and loss, the absence of healthy adults feeds the growth of gangs. Gangs are magnets for young people in search of connection, security, safety, respect, love, and identity. Once gangs gain a significant presence in a community, fear, intimidation, and necessity add to the pressure on young people to participate in gang life.

    In Chelsea, for example, 11 percent of the high school students report associations with gangs, but this represents only a fraction of the young people who are affected, involved, or influenced by gangs. In the 1990s, many of the local gangs were Asian and were formed in response to challenges from groups of Whites, Latinos, and African Americans. Asian gangs are now overshadowed by the competing Central American gangs, which have gained strength from immigration patterns over the last decade.

    Indeed, U.S. immigration policies play a major role in how gangs form and spread in cities like Chelsea.[8] During the 1990s, young Salvadoreans fleeing the violence of civil war became embroiled in the gang dynamics of the barrios of Los Angeles. They formed ethnically based gangs such as the Salvadorean Mara Salvatrucha or MS-13 and the 18th Street gang. Since the 1996 Immigration Law was enacted, U.S. law enforcement has deported illegal immigrants and foreign-born American citizens who were charged with even minor offenses, including petty theft or disorderly conduct. Between 2000 and 2004, the U.S. government sent an estimated 20,000 young Central Americans—all raised in the United States—back to these countries. Essentially, immigration authorities exported American gang violence to poor communities in Central America, where youth under the age of fifteen represent 45 percent of the population.

Communities with substantial immigrant populations from Central America are now drawn into a vicious cycle. Young people abandoned by war-torn adults are recruited into gangs, which then circulate between these countries and the communities of the north. Incarceration within both U.S. prisons and the jails of Central America further cements gang loyalty and identification. It also fuels the vicious violence that engulfs communities within these countries as well as U.S. communities, such as Chelsea and East Boston.

Many smaller local gangs are now loosely associated with the nationally identified colors of the Crips and Bloods in a shifting and confusing set of alliances that only adds to the endemic sense of insecurity. Although originally formed along ethnic lines, many gangs include Asians, Latinos, Whites, and Blacks. Nor are they bound geographically to specific neighborhoods. Gang conflicts traverse the region. A young person in Revere is beaten up by a group that drove over from East Boston. Tagging in one city is done by a group from another. ("Tagging" marks territory or "turf" by putting a gang's name on a public space to inform other gangs of their presence.) At Roca, members from seven or eight actively hostile gangs participate in activities, generally coexisting peaceably within the oasis of Roca itself. Yet traveling to and from Roca is treacherous, often discouraging young people from participating in the center's programs at all.

The Clarity of Roca: All Young People Belong

American culture has a powerful tendency to blame the victim. Not surprisingly, then, young people who face the awesome "monsters" of modern life often find themselves being treated as if they themselves were the monsters. Youth are seen as the problem that needs fixing, the source of community dysfunction. By this logic, youth become the target of massive adult intervention to control, minimize, repress, and repair their many perceived deficits.

Roca sees young people differently. It views its work as accompanying young people on their journey toward adulthood. Roca workers therefore seek to support and nurture the positive development of youth as they face the many monsters that society sets before them. Perhaps most important, Roca helps communities build their capacity to help all young people grow in healthy ways.

> "It is really easy to get into a place where you think of young people as needing policing. Young people don't need policing; they need relationships."
>
> SAYRA, ROCA STAFF

Roca's stance on helping young people is consistent with the philosophy of positive youth development: young people and their dreams, identity, voice, and power are the solution, not the problem. This positive approach is key to understanding why Roca adopted the peacemaking Circle as a core tool in its work with young people. In other words, before Roca could know for sure that peacemaking Circles would be of such value to them in their work, they needed to be clear about their mission with young people and communities.

In the years before adopting Circles, Roca worked hard to become an organization that was clear about its values, vision, mission, and methods. As important and powerful as peacemaking Circles are, they are simply a means for Roca to accomplish its mission. Roca's purpose is neither to practice Circles nor to promote them. Rather, the peacemaking Circle process—with its emphasis on the fundamental values of respect, human development, and mutual accountability—gives Roca a strategic method to help young people and the community be who they really are. Roca needed to clarify its vision of the world, its mission as an organization, its core values, and its most useful methods. To achieve these levels of organizational self-awareness and clarity, Roca had to become an organization capable of learning.

Being a Learning Organization

> "The fundamental difference between creating and problem solving is simple. In problem solving, we seek to make something we do not like go away. In creating, we seek to make what we truly care about exist. Few distinctions are more basic."
>
> PETER SENGE[9]

At Roca, the mission, vision, and values are not fancy words that adorn stationery or plaques to be dragged out once or twice a year and paraded before funders. Rather, clarity of vision and mission shapes the strategies that Roca chooses to pursue every day. It helps Roca keep in view what is sacred and what is not. It guides the staff when they need to make difficult choices about what is most important for the organization. Commitment to core values gives the organization guidance and direction, and it also defines the kind of outcomes that Roca expects to see in the lives of young people.

In other words, attending to its development as an organization has kept Roca on course. Daily distractions can sap energies, and monumental pressures could easily divert the organization from its chosen focus. Becoming a learning organization—and sustaining itself as one—helps Roca stay true to its purpose despite these pressures. As a learning organization, Roca continually strives to be *intentional* about its purpose and the methods it uses to achieve its goals.

Roca discovered organizational development the hard way. Molly Baldwin openly admits that when she founded Roca in 1988, she had no idea what it meant to build and develop an organization. "There were so many times I got myself into trouble, and people would say, you know organizations have development processes, . . . and I would say, 'They do? Gee, couldn't you have told me this before?'"

In 1992, for example, Roca wanted to set up a storefront on Shirley Avenue in the heart of the Cambodian community. As they contemplated this expansion, they wanted to be clear about what they were doing and why. Key staff expressed a desire to hold themselves to a common purpose beyond their personal agendas. Furthermore, they wanted this purpose to be rooted in the shared understandings of Roca's staff, young people, and the wider community.

Molly Baldwin, Roca's
executive director, and
Angie Rodriguez,
Roca staff

With help from a number of coaches and mentors, the staff and young people at Roca set out to become what organizational theorists call a "learning organization." This meant, among other things, that Roca had to be transparent in its decision-making. It also had to be continually self-reflective not only about its own performance but also about its value to young people and to the communities of Chelsea and Revere.

> "So if organizations are collections of human beings coming together to do something that hopefully means something, how do you not make it about a person or a group of people or whatever drama we are going through this week? It's really easy to get caught in drama or to do stupid things. And I'm a really strong person. That's good news for the organization and bad news for the organization. So the way to supersede me or any other strong leader—to supercede our personalities, character flaws, and passions—is to be about something bigger and to hold yourself to something bigger."
>
> MOLLY, ROCA'S EXECUTIVE DIRECTOR

The emphasis on ongoing evaluation at Roca reflects its moral commitment to hold itself accountable to the young people and the community: Does Roca deliver on its promises? Organizations are means to ends, not ends in themselves. Roca deeply believes that, as an organization, it must continually ask itself if what it does has value to the young people within the communities it serves. It must also learn how to use tools of measurement, so it can not only justify the investment of funders but also answer these questions for itself.

> "Well, the question is, what are we doing here? Is it any good? Is it of value? Does it matter to people?

That's about meaning and purpose. And I think that's
what the mission, vision, and values do for us. Our
values are our outcomes—they are the same. Does
what we do mean anything? How do you know that
something is of value? How do you know if what
you're doing is good?"

MOLLY, ROCA'S EXECUTIVE DIRECTOR

These questions speak to Roca's vision of what its organization is
all about. One feature of learning organizations is that they build
on shared visions. This is certainly true of Roca. By continually
posing vision-oriented questions, Roca has become continually
innovative about its activities and programs. The drive toward
innovation leads Roca to form relationships with other organizations and institutions that work with young people. Rejecting
the approach that treats young people as problems that must be
solved, Roca strives to create a better world by tapping the power
of young people.

The work at Roca is therefore a creative enterprise. It constantly explores new ways to generate positive opportunities and
environments for young people. Building on a vision of a just
community where all young people thrive, Roca strives to harness
the creative capacity and will of the larger community to change
how it responds to youth. By collaborating with other organizations involved with the young people's lives, Roca has been the
catalyst for broad systemic change—within institutions, governments, and systems.

In all of these organization-changing processes, the Circle has
served as a key tool. Circles create a context that supports visioning, values, and change. According to Molly, the Circle process
was the single most important tool that helped Roca *practice* the
art of organizational learning and development. Although Roca
learned a great deal from mentors and coaches about what to do
as an organization, it was the Circle that provided a context and

method for Roca staff to hold each other to the values they shared and to their common purpose. Thus, one of the most unexpected developments for Roca as an organization—and for several of the institutions that have been exposed to the Circle through working with Roca—has been the use of Circles as a tool for organizational learning.

Roca's Core Values

Roca's mission is to promote justice by creating opportunities for young people to lead happy and healthy lives. Roca does this by exploring ways to help young people experience four core values:

- belonging,
- generosity,
- competence,
- independence.

Inspired by a model of youth development rooted in Indigenous principles, these four core values guide every aspect of Roca's approach to youth development.[10] Indeed, Roca relies on these four values not only to shape their concept of what young people need to thrive and lead change but also to measure the outcomes of their work. Both the staff and the organization as a whole hold themselves accountable for helping to bring these four values into young people's lives on a daily basis.

Underlying all their work, Roca operates from a core premise: *belonging*. At Roca, everyone is welcomed; everyone belongs. Roca is unconditionally in relationship with all people, especially young people, in the community. What does this mean? Disenfranchised people are excluded from most public and private institutions as well as from many physical spaces in society. This is especially true for young people, poor people, immigrants, and other newcomers who lack resources. Belonging is conditional: if you do not fit certain criteria, you are not welcome. Opportunities come with caveats: if you cannot meet certain requirements, doors will close.

So it is for the young people who find a place at Roca. They have been chronically excluded from almost every other social space, including their own homes, schools (public, alternative, and private), foster homes, traditional youth and youth development programs, retail stores, malls, city parks, public streets, and, indeed, American soil itself. They lack "eligibility" for all kinds of programs and privileges, and the few entitlements they have are easily rescinded as soon as they make a mistake or fail to do something right. They quite literally do not have a place where they can "be."

Roca is committed to working with the young people and community members who are the least likely to show up because they have been lost in the margins of society. Regardless of the young people's nonconformity with rules and social norms or lack of fit with the opportunity structure of mainstream society, Roca relentlessly persists in staying connected with the youth. The relationship is unconditional, which means, quite simply, that Roca does not give up on anyone. At Roca, belonging is based on the understanding that all people have value, are important, and are worthy of love. Roca's premise is that when individuals or communities share a sense of belonging, they are more able to embrace values such as respect, love, and a commitment to mutual safety.

Generosity is about developing a sense of purpose and value by giving of ourselves—from our souls and spirits. Roca believes that all people have the ability to contribute to their community and to appreciate how meaningful their contribution is. Everyone has something to offer that is truly needed by others. Giving of who we are brings a sense of empowerment and self-determination. It enables individuals and communities not only to get healthy themselves but also to collaborate in promoting the larger social good.

As individuals or communities practice generosity, they learn how to express other values as well: love, faith, peace, hope, humility, integrity, and empathy. Roca has found that when young people experience belonging and generosity on a regular basis, they begin to act in ways that support a healthier lifestyle. They attend school, show up on time, take care of their bodies, treat others respectfully, and set goals.

In addition to belonging and generosity, Roca intentionally cultivates two other values that are essential to healthy human development. All of Roca's programming seeks to build competencies for young people. *Competence* is about developing skills—mentally, emotionally, and physically. Young people who experience a sense of competence feel able to face challenges and to help others to do the same. For both young people and community members, Roca creates opportunities for learning and development that are not then suddenly "closed" whenever someone makes a mistake. Building competence reduces youth's fears about being able to cope with life and its challenges. At the same time, it vastly enhances a young person's sense of security, self-esteem, trust, and well-being.

The fourth value is *independence*. A growing sense of competence builds independence. Independence is about self-determination and leadership. It's about knowing how to live out of harm's way, become self-sufficient, and conduct oneself responsibly. When young people experience independence, they articulate a vision for themselves and take steps to work toward that vision. Gaining a sense of independence promotes values of responsibility, determination, leadership, commitment, and accountability. And it brings many benefits. With independence comes, for example, emotional strength and the inner resources to face obstacles. The capacity to collaborate with others expands. Exercising personal autonomy energizes people. Young people start taking realistic, concrete actions toward creating a different future for themselves. In the process, they gain confidence, knowing that they can do this throughout their lifetimes.

Roca's four core values also serve as its core outcomes. That is, Roca uses these four values to realize its vision—a world where young people thrive and lead change for themselves and their communities. By practicing and modeling the values in how Roca's staff relates to all its community members, Roca instills these values in young people. In turn, the youth embrace the values and learn how to practice them in their own lives. In other words, by promoting experiences of belonging, generosity, competence, and independence among young people, Roca empowers them to play their roles in creating a just world.

This model of "being there" for youth is not a therapeutic technique or a specialized set of skills; rather, it is a way to be with oneself and others in the world. This worldview is formed through a strong connection with an Indigenous worldview. Based on the Medicine Wheel, this worldview teaches about the interconnectedness of life and how all life follows cyclical patterns.[11] In Roca's experience, this model emerged from actually being in relationship with young people, as they struggled to create healthy and sustainable lives for themselves in the face of systemic global injustice and oppression.

Living "problem-free" is not, then, the purpose. Instead, the mission is to promote justice by creating opportunities for all people to thrive and lead change. The lens Roca has chosen to view young people and their families does not focus on deficits. Each and every young person is viewed as a source of value and strength. Young people, their families, and their communities are the solution, not the problem.

CHAPTER THREE

The Circle as a Strategy in Youth Development

"It takes having a sense of belonging, generosity, competence, and independence to walk the road of change."

SPEAKER AT ROCA'S FIFTEENTH ANNIVERSARY CELEBRATION

Roca's mission is to promote justice by creating opportunities for young people to become self-sufficient and live out of harm's way. To pursue this mission, Roca uses five strategic methods designed to increase the positive outcomes for young people and their communities. Each strategy integrates the four values as much as possible. These five strategies are

1. Engaging youth through streetwork and outreach;
2. Building transformational relationships;
3. Using peacemaking Circles;
4. Creating opportunities in education, employment, and civic participation;
5. Working with institutions related to the youth, such as social services, the criminal justice system, educational institutions, health services, and places of employment.

A strategy is a method for fulfilling an organization's mission. While strategies are important, they are only the means to actualize a goal. Even so, it is easy to confuse an organization's strategy with its mission. Often organizations focus a great deal of attention on their methods—that they use a certain kind of therapy, for example, or teach young people a particular skill—when it is far more important for them to be clear about the purpose for using a strategy.

At Roca, programs and strategies evolve and change, but they always develop within the context of Roca's overarching purpose. The discipline of being a learning organization helps Roca ensure that each of its strategies and programs serves its mission. Programs may shift and strategies change, but Roca's commitment to its mission, vision, and values remains steady.

All of Roca's "strategic methods" are about building relationships. This core element is both simple and profoundly challenging. No specialized curriculum or high-level expertise underlies these strategies. Roca's methods do not require expensive technology or massive resources. Through each of its methods, Roca aspires to be "brilliantly ordinary." Roca coined this phrase to capture an important idea: everyone has the ability to do the "work" of Roca. At the heart of Roca's strategic methods is simply the commitment to building and practicing relationships based on core values—most clearly, the value of love.

Showing Up on the Street

At first, the young men from a Central American gang eye with suspicion the stranger clad in the distinctive purple jacket. George is a thirty-year-old streetworker born in Puerto Rico and raised in Chelsea. Every day, George is out on the streets, looking for the chance to build connection and relationship with young men and women ready for change. It is George's job to pay particular attention to this group of Salvadorean young men. They ask him questions, trying to figure out who he is and what he wants. They push him away and tell him to get lost, but the next day, like clockwork, he is back.

This is how the dance begins. Slowly, wearing his purple jacket with the name of Roca blazoned in bright yellow on the back, George becomes a familiar figure. One day, he shows up with the van: Anyone want to play soccer? Go fishing? Hear some music, or get some food? Slowly, George works his strategy: he knows he must make a connection with the leaders in their late twenties in order to gain access to the younger ones, like fifteen-year-old Edgar, who has traveled from El Salvador to join his older brother on the streets of Chelsea. George knows he must work with the dynamics of the gang to help those who want to find a way out. The group must see him as non-threatening, someone safe to talk to. If they see him joking with the leaders, they might begin to feel that they can do the same. It is a delicate and sometimes dangerous dance.

Young Edgar is ready. He starts to join George on trips to Roca. Then Edgar takes a huge risk and shows up at Roca on his own. For months, he comes to Roca and won't talk with anyone but George. Still, he continues to show up for a meal or a game of soccer. Inside Roca, the staff watches for opportunities to build relationships with Edgar. They take note of his needs: Does he have food, sufficient clothing, a place to sleep? What is his emotional state? Is he learning? What about his spiritual life? Invitations are made over and over: Want to lift weights? Come to an ESL class? Talk to the doctor at the clinic? Attend a service? Come to a performance? Learn to break dance? The goal at Roca is to promote young people, so that they thrive. The strategy is to build relationships that promote self-sufficiency and positive growth for young people like Edgar. Always and intentionally, the conversation is about growth.

Long before Roca was housed in a building, the work of Roca took place wherever young people were found: in the park, on the beach, behind the movie house, on the front stoop, in the school-yard, or in the house. For years, Roca was no more than a store-front, a home base for activities that took place on the street. Today, despite outward appearances, the activities of streetwork and outreach remain a central method for Roca. The work contin-ues to be about what takes place outside of the building, not just what goes on inside.

> When Saroeum Phoung first met Molly, he was seventeen years old. His mother had enrolled him in a private Catholic school in Boston, but despite all her efforts, Saroeum was deep into gang life with a crew he had formed with his friends. He actually liked school: he painted and wrote poetry, but the gang was his home. When a friend at the school told Molly about him, Molly showed up on the basketball court in Revere late at night and introduced herself.

What does it mean to be from the street? It does not necessarily mean being homeless, in a gang, undocumented, or out of school, although many of those who are "on the street" fit these descrip-tions. The "street" is a metaphor for a sense of belonging that arises from an even more powerful sense of exclusion from other spaces in society. Young people on the street may live at home or attend school, but they exist on the margins of those spaces and have detached or difficult relationships with family mem-bers, teachers, and other adults. They seek the company of other young people in similar situations, and the more they identify with these relationships and are motivated by them, the more they are involved in the life of the street.

> "I felt like I got lost between two identities when I got involved in the gang. Your family rejects you when

you join a gang. And then you go out on the street, and society rejects you. . . . It started out as a racial thing. You come to this country, and people look at you differently. Treat you like dirt. It makes you feel hopeless. So now where do people turn? Like me, I turned to a gang. These guys grew up in the same place and had the same experience. . . . We would get together and talk about Cambodia. . . . We used Cambodian and American street language. . . . In a way, in the gang, we created our own culture. . . . I wish I didn't have to go through the gang stuff in order to . . . find that love among ourselves."

SAROEUM, ROCA STAFF[1]

Streetwork and outreach intentionally build a different kind of relationship with youth and young adults—a relationship that can push youth into leading positive change for themselves. Roca's streetworkers engage young people who have been "abandoned" by the developmental institutions, and they treat each young person as a precious human being. The essence of streetwork and outreach is to recognize young people as worthy members of the community and to begin to build relationships with them that can transform both the young people and their communities.

"Molly didn't see me as a parent would—their kid drinking on the street. She was looking at my brain. I wasn't just a figure of me being on the street. I was a figure of a young person who has a lot of talent."

SAROEUM, ROCA STAFF[2]

Streetworkers engage young people by showing up for them. They give them their phone numbers—work, home, and cell; they let them know where they live; and they meet with the youth in their own houses, even if it is late at night or on weekends. "Showing up" in Roca's sense means being a consistent presence in the life of a young person, above and beyond what it takes to deliver specific services. It involves an abiding commitment to being there for young people in whatever ways they may need support. Most fundamentally, it means interacting with them positively— seeing them as more than just a source of trouble or dysfunction in the community.

Physically, streetworkers go wherever young people are. They visit isolated young moms at home. They call them regularly. If a baby is ill, they accompany a mom to the doctor or visit them in the hospital. A streetworker might meet regularly with a group of young gang members where they routinely hang out in someone's basement or front stoop. Every morning, streetworkers go to the courthouse to talk to young people who are facing charges or who are there to meet with their probation officers. When someone gets locked up, they visit, write, and send socks or food. Streetworkers head out in Roca vans and spend several hours picking up young people who are willing to come to an activity at Roca. They are on the street at night in the places where young people gather and out in force at street festivals or soccer games. Roca is a presence in the community. People in the community know Roca, and they know that it is Roca's job to know young people. In the dense, tightly packed streets of this small city, Roca's distinctive purple and yellow jackets are recognized throughout the community.

> "What matters is showing up—physically being
> there—on the street . . . putting in extra time on the
> weekend out of working time. . . . When you show
> up on the weekend or spend some one-on-one time,
> taking them out for something to eat, checking up on
> them, or checking in on them, that's when they begin
> to open up."
>
> VICHEY, ROCA STAFF

This relationship begins in the comfort zone of the young person, wherever that might be. At first, the relationship may consist of no more than a persistent greeting, a few friendly words exchanged every day. From Roca's perspective, the timeline for building the relationship is indefinite, because the relationship is unconditional. Roca does not give up on a person if a relationship is slow to develop. Persistence and patience are important attributes of streetwork: showing up again and again is the foundation for being real with young people.

Roca knows from experience, for example, that a two-word greeting can grow into a couple sentences exchanged, then a willingness to come to an event, to talk to more people, to join an activity, and eventually to drop in at the building. Trust builds slowly as the relationship grows, and that relationship becomes the leverage for even greater personal change. Because Roca strives to be a rock—a constant presence in the lives of young people in the community—Roca imposes no arbitrary time limits on how long it might take for the relationship to develop. The invitation remains open for whenever the individual is ready.

> "I didn't put my trust in her [Molly] right away, because there were other people who had tried to help me from other programs. But then she kept showing up while I'm on the street drinking a forty. She would show up in the middle of the night. I mean, this lady used to call me at school to see if I was there. I had a beeper then, so she used to beep me, and she gave me all her numbers to call. I really hated her at the time. I felt like taking a gun and blowing her head off. I didn't see that she was helping me. One of the things that did help is that she persevered."
>
> SAROEUM, ROCA STAFF[3]

Developing the Transformational Relationship (TR)

> *Charles was twelve when he lost his older brother to suicide.*
> *Just two months later, he lost his mother to AIDS. When he*
> *began to show up at Roca, his reputation in the community*
> *was already well established: police, social services, schools,*
> *and young people all said Charles was "crazy." No school held*
> *him for long, his grandparents could not control him, the*
> *police had him pegged as a kid with "mental issues" and a*
> *"troublemaker." Whenever Charles came into Roca, before the*
> *day was over, he would provoke a fight or outburst that would*
> *result in his being asked to leave the building.*

At Roca, the transformational relationship juxtaposes two apparently contradictory attitudes that the staff maintains toward young people. Standards of behavior are unyieldingly high, while support and love remain unconditional. In this case, even though Charles's behavior constantly led to his being asked to leave the building, Charles was never asked to leave Roca. The next day, he was always expected to come back and try again.

> *Victor Jose is a soft-spoken man born in the Dominican Repub-*
> *lic and raised in Chelsea. Charles formed a connection with*
> *Victor. Each time Charles came to Roca, Victor greeted him:*
> *"How are you? How is school? What's going on?" At first,*
> *Charles didn't answer. For months, he'd talk to kids but never*
> *to adults. Still, Victor reached out, asking questions, observ-*
> *ing what Charles liked, and offering activities or food.*
>
> *Slowly, Charles began to participate. And each time Charles*
> *"blew up," provoked a fight, or acted out, Victor had a consis-*
> *tent response: you are loved, you are accepted, but this is what*
> *is expected of you. Victor would bring him to his office and*
> *talk about what is acceptable and what is not, what Roca is*
> *going to hold him accountable for while he was in there in the*

space at Roca. Sometimes Victor would offer alternative ways to express his frustration and anger: let's go outside and run, let's go dance or draw. Each day, Victor would tell Charles that, although he couldn't stay there any longer that day, he wanted him to come back tomorrow and try again. And each day, Charles returned to try again. Gradually, Charles learned how to be at Roca without getting into fights or yelling and screaming at other kids. Incidents grew further and further apart, as Charles came to feel he belonged at Roca.

Victor also formed relationships with the other adults in Charles's life. Neither Charles's grandmother nor any school could "hold" Charles. For nearly a year, Charles was not enrolled in school at all. He was constantly on the run from home and a string of foster homes. Charles was trapped in an institutional vortex: his grandmother didn't want him in a foster home, but she complained to the courts that she was fearful of him and could not control him. Charles was removed and put in placement. After running from there, he would be arrested and put in lockup for a few days before being sent back home to grandma. Grandma would show up in court and refuse to take him back home, and the cycle would begin again.

For a while, Charles was locked up in a DYS (Department of Youth Services) facility, but he was too young to be there for long, his only crime being that he ran away. Invariably, when Charles ran, he ran to Roca. Although Charles could not live at Roca, for him, Roca was a place where he felt at home. Each time Charles showed up at Roca, Victor would contact the police. The trajectory of this downward spiral was all too familiar for those who work with young, marginalized people. Victor knew that without significant intervention, Charles would eventually be locked up for good.

Victor started to build a strong relationship with Charles's grandmother, making home visits to get to know her better.

Soon she and Charles's aunt were calling Victor to talk about Charles. Victor built connections with Charles's DSS (Department of Social Services) worker and the schools. Both institutions started calling Victor to try and figure out what to do about Charles.

When Charles confided to Victor that he was a victim of sexual abuse, Victor believed him. Then, when Charles was assaulted by a family member in Victor's presence, Victor took action on his behalf. Building on his solid relationships with the family, the DSS workers, the police, and the schools, Victor succeeded in finding Charles a placement in a residential school where he would have twenty-four-hour supervision and the emotional support he needed to do well.

For the first time, Charles did not run away or blow out of the school. He wrote and called Victor to tell him how happy he was there. The first place Charles visited when he came home for Christmas was Roca.

Transformational relationships are long-term, trusting relationships. At Roca, these relationships are mostly between youth and adults. However, transformational relationships can also form between two youth as well as between two adults. A transformational relationship functions as a catalyst for change. It combines support and challenge in a way that promotes personal growth and development.

The transformational relationship centers on the twin forces of accountability and unconditional love. Victor consistently and repeatedly told Charles he loved him. He consistently repeated the message that nothing Charles could do would change the way he felt about him. Yet, he also consistently held Charles accountable for high standards of conduct within Roca. Slowly, Charles responded. He learned how to manage his anger and negative behavior. His outbursts diminished as he began to pursue positive activities.

The nature of the transformational relationship builds on

Roca's model of growth and change. Promoting positive change within a young person is Roca's overriding goal, and transformational relationships provide one essential means for this change to happen. Positive change is an uncomfortable process. It involves incremental steps, setbacks, and non-linear leaps. People gradually abandon one set of habits, attitudes, and feelings to replace them with a different set of behaviors, attitudes, and feelings. Because change is so unpredictable, making a change requires that we take risks. Yet, to do that, we need support. The transformational relationship serves as both a catalyst and a safety zone. It supports youth as they take many small steps toward new ways of being in the world.

At Roca, building these kinds of relationships with young people is one of the core strategies for doing the work of youth and community development. The transformational relationship begins with outreach and streetwork and then develops along a continuum. From the staff's point of view, developing a transformational relationship has different phases. During the outreach phase, Roca's staff members work on building trust with the young person and getting him or her involved. The young person is continually invited to come to Roca to attend an event, go to class, play soccer, drop by for Circle, have a bite to eat, or play basketball. At some point, the young person accepts the invitation and begins to participate more at Roca on his or her own initiative. This is an important signal that staff members watch for: the young person is taking the lead in making changes and is ready for more. At this point, he or she is in a transformational relationship with a staff member.

The model of the transformational relationship is similar to mentoring in some respects. Both arise from recognizing the importance of adults in the lives of youth, particularly disadvantaged youth. In studies of youth resiliency, those who thrive despite difficult experiences often have caring, non-parent adults present in their lives. This is the founding insight of both mentoring programs and Roca. When Molly Baldwin set out to row on the Charles River with pregnant teens, she knew the purpose of the outing had little to do with rowing and everything to do with the emotional connection between struggling adolescents and a caring adult. The active ingredient in both mentoring and transformational relationships is a close, trusting connection.

But the model of transformational relationships at Roca differs from mentoring models in important ways. Nearly two million American youth participate in mentoring programs where they meet with a Big Brother or Big Sister an average of three times per month. These adult volunteers are matched with a young person by paid staff who supervise and train the volunteer mentors. The mentors spend a certain amount of time with each young person, taking them out to lunch, going to a ball game, or just hanging out.

Research on mentoring programs reveals some of the strengths and weaknesses of these relationships.[4] When mentoring works well, the chemistry is strong between the young person and the mentor. Their interactions are consistent, and the relationship lasts for a substantial length of time, at least one year or more. Mentoring is most successful when the young person is veering toward trouble but still on the edge, not in so deep that he or she has dropped out of school, become active in gangs, or been involved with the criminal justice system.

Mentoring is often less successful with youth who have been exposed to emotional or sexual abuse or those with behavioral and psychological problems. These youth are often too distrustful to build a relationship with a volunteer mentor, who may not "hang in" long enough to overcome the youth's deep-seated distrust of adults. Furthermore, traditional mentoring is more successful with younger youth (ages ten to twelve) and far more difficult to sustain with older teens (ages thirteen to sixteen). Very few mentoring programs target young people older than sixteen.

Successful mentoring requires consistency and accountability from the mentor. If a mentor fails to maintain the relationship, the experience can have a negative impact on the young person, particularly among youth who have been disappointed by significant adults before. In fact, research shows that a negative experience with a mentor affects a young person's sense of self and behavior more than the positive outcomes from a good experience. The disappointment, loss, and rejection from a relationship that is unreliable, judgmental, or harmful can prove devastating to vulnerable youth, who may have been better off left alone.

Roca deals with young people unlikely to qualify for or benefit from typical mentoring programs. These young people are older—in their late teens and twenties. They are more seriously at risk due to a host of more challenging life circumstances, including substance abuse, gang involvement, psychological trauma, single parenthood, school failure, and involvement with the criminal justice system. The outreach phase at Roca's work is often so lengthy, because it is hard to build connections with young people who have become profoundly distrustful of adults and mainstream institutions. Without the leverage of trusting relationships that begin out on the street, young people most likely would never show up at Roca at all.

Roca does not use volunteers to build transformational relationships with young people. Building transformational relationships is the work of paid staff, because it demands intense levels of contact between the staff and the young person. Generally, the "match" at Roca between a staff member and a young person is organic: a young person will gravitate toward a particular staff person during the early phase of outreach. The growing bond between them becomes the magnet that draws the young person to Roca and keeps them coming back.

While all adults at Roca are engaged in relationship-building with young people, the responsibility of being in a transformational relationship is deep and not taken lightly. Staff members commit to young people, person-to-person, which means that they pay attention to them and their progress. They talk to them about their lives and their future and actively look for opportunities to support their growth. They monitor, acknowledge, and reward their progress. They get to know their family, friends, girlfriends, boyfriends, probation officers, teachers, and social workers. They make it their business to build connections with all the people in the young people's lives, so they can advocate for them and support them.

Roca's staff and streetworkers understand that the change process involves ups and downs and many setbacks, which are inevitably disheartening and frustrating. They are prepared for this process and recognize it as part of the normal rhythm of growth and change. They understand that their role is precisely not to give up when the young person pushes them away or returns to old habits. While the relationship is mutual in affection and highly personal, there is no confusion about the locus of responsibility, which lies with the adults to support the young people as they grow. When young people act out or fail to show up—which they do over and over—the staff person pursues them again and again.

> "A good chunk of the time, they are angry with you.
> A good chunk of the time, it is not about laughing and
> giggling and all that. It's not one of those relationships
> where it's nice and everyone just gets along. That's not
> what a TR (transformational relationship) is. It's the
> tough stuff. It's about getting into what it means to
> live in the world and helping young people to under-
> stand that they deserve to be in the world and that in
> order to get there, they need to do certain things."
>
> SUSAN, ROCA STAFF

As with mentoring, the psychological value of these relationships for young people is the opportunity to see themselves and their futures differently. They have a chance to see themselves through the eyes of another person. Roca staff members talk with youth about the future and encourage them to look honestly at their current lives. As the youth grow in their awareness, they become motivated to take action to close the gap between where they are and where they would like to be.

To build this critical awareness, Roca has developed a range of methods and opportunities that get young people to talk about themselves: their lives, their values, and their physical, mental, emotional, and spiritual well-being. As young people explore these dimensions, they build their self-awareness, their communication skills, as well as their trust with the larger adult world. They also gain a clearer sense both of what they need to do in their lives and of the kinds of relationships they want to build with others.

> "For me, the TR is about trust, it's about friendship, but it is also so clearly about being able to hold people accountable—being able to say, what are you doing, and why? What's going on that you are behaving like this?—and then to have them actually be able to address you with an answer. They may storm out, but if you're in a serious TR, they will come back. And if they don't come back, you go out and get 'em . . . and then they'll come back."
>
> SUSAN, ROCA STAFF

Staff members in transformational relationships with young people look for signs of readiness for a further step. The relationship itself becomes a source of momentum and support for positive personal change. It pushes youth to alter their patterns. The relationship builds this capacity—this power—through consistent contact, modeling, strategic support, trust, and meaningful dialogue.

By investing the time it takes to know and love these young people, staff members earn the right to push them to grow. Roca does not rely on threats, punishments, or the coercion of the courts to hold young people to high standards. It is the connection that Roca staff members build with youth and the trust that goes with those relationships that give the staff the leverage to hold young people to high expectations—to encourage them to find "new ways of being" in the world and to support them in developing these new behaviors.

> "And so it's a balancing act between all these things. . . . It's about teaching young people—who oftentimes don't have parents—what it means to have values and morals . . . because out on the street, it's a very different code, a different way of life, so that . . . it's sort of re-parenting and re-educating all at the same time."
>
> SUSAN, ROCA STAFF

Like mentors, the adult staff serve as both role models and advocates. As advocates, they are fundamentally on the side of the young person, helping them negotiate and deal with the other people in their lives. As role models, more than anything else, the staff person models accountability. This is extremely important for youth who have experienced enormous instability and failure from adults in their families and community. Modeling consistency, reliability, persistence, and patience is critical. Again, in its founding vision, Roca aspires to be a rock in the lives of young people who have been cast adrift by the adult world. The transformational relationship must be a steady presence in the life of a young person.

> "They have been lied to a lot, and they are not used to people keeping their word, so the first important action is to keep our word no matter what. When we say we are going to do something, we do it."
>
> MEHRNOUSH, ROCA STAFF WORKER

The transformational relationship is, therefore, neither a professionalized service nor a therapeutic relationship. While mentoring and other kinds of social services (e.g., education, treatment, and vocational and professional assistance) play important roles in youth development, these services are no substitute for the core transformational relationship. In fact, without the deeper affective ties—the emotional bonds—of the transformational relationship, these services are likely to go unutilized.

As Molly observes, "We can get a young person a job, but two weeks later he blows out of it. And we can keep finding him a job over and over, but what will make him show up every day? What will make him go on to college and do what it takes to find a better job?" The depth of internal transformation that many young people need requires a different catalyst. At Roca, the key instigator of change has been the one-on-one relationship. This bond creates the emotional space in which a youth's personal transformation becomes possible.

Coming Together in Peacemaking Circles

At the time he began to hang out at Roca, Luis already had numerous drug charges pending at court. As a gang leader, he was well known to the police and had not been in school since his expulsion from eleventh grade. As Luis floated in and out of Roca, he began to develop relationships with two Roca streetworkers: Jasson, a young Salvadorean streetworker who worked with many young men who were gang involved, and Norman, an older African American streetworker, who regularly showed up at the courthouse to talk with youth facing charges.

As these relationships grew, Luis started to show up regularly at Roca to lift weights. Inside the weight room, he talked with Jasson about his life and his participation in gangs. Roca requires all young people to refrain from signing, clothing, and language associated with gangs while in the building, and Luis respected these rules. He and Jasson talked about what he was doing with his life, and whether or not this was what he really wanted.

Luis asked Jasson to help him organize a Circle in order to negotiate a truce among rival gangs locked in an escalating spiral of retaliation and violence. Together, Jasson and Luis organized a Circle between his gang and a major rival gang. The purpose of the Circle was to create an agreement between the two gangs to reduce violence out on the streets. At that Circle, Luis stood up and offered apologies for the harm his gang had caused and pledged his commitment to ending hostilities.

After the Circle, Jasson and Norman persuaded Luis to attend a four-day Circle training at Roca. During those four days, in the presence of adults and other young people, Luis shared his sense of despair with the life he was living and his growing desire to leave the street. His behavior began to change more radically: he arrived at Roca early in the morning and remained in the building all day. He attended classes, volunteered with younger kids, and started going to church. Norman helped him move into a transitional housing program away from his old neighborhood, so he could be apart from the most intense gang activity. He talked openly with people about his plans to be finished with the gangs, go back to high school, and one day attend college.

Late one night, inspired by the Circles at Roca, Luis organized his own Circle in a park in the middle of Chelsea. To the young men, this meeting was a continuation of the Circle inside Roca, but to police, this was a dangerous gathering of some of the most troublesome and violent gang members within the city. A neighbor alerted the police, who arrived to search, disperse, or arrest any with outstanding warrants. Drugs were found, charges filed, and Luis landed with a serious charge of *possession within a school zone. Despite recent changes in his life, the trajectory of his past caught up with him.*

Still, Luis did not lose hope. With the support of people from Roca and the community, Luis continued to make positive changes in his life. Three months later when his case came to trial, Luis was convicted and sentenced to a mandatory two years in jail. The blow was devastating.

At sentencing, the judge gave Luis a stay for one week before starting his time. Luis resisted the powerful temptation to run and instead reached out to people at Roca to help him cope with the prospect of going to jail. Prisons are overwhelmingly negative environments that often instigate personal bitterness and anger inside those already stuck in negative patterns of behavior. Luis asked for a Circle to help him find the courage and determination to face what lay ahead.

Roca organized a series of support Circles for Luis. In these Circles, people in the community who had met him in Circle along with Roca's staff helped Luis focus on his primary goals for his life. They encouraged him to make the most of his time behind the wall, so he could continue his journey toward a better life. They shared stories of their own struggles, their own experiences with loss, disappointment, and obstacles. They shared wisdom from their own time in jail and the experiences of people like Malcolm X, who had used incarceration as a place to work toward positive ends.

Once on the inside, it was clear that Luis was unlike most young inmates at the Suffolk County House of Correction. He attended GED classes, took care of himself physically, went to church, and regularly exchanged letters and visits with Roca staff and community members from the support Circle. Although behind the wall, Luis remained a part of Roca.

Peacemaking Circles are integral to everything Roca does not only with young people and adults in the community but also with

managing and developing its own organization. Peacemaking
Circles are a way of communicating derived from Aboriginal and
Native traditions. Based on the principles of the Medicine Wheel,
the peacemaking Circle embodies democratic, egalitarian, and
spiritual values. It is an intentionally sacred space that removes
barriers and opens opportunities for people to acknowledge and
connect with each other. Within the Circle, people leave behind the
roles and positions that otherwise divide and stratify us. Everyone
comes simply as a human being.

Young people, parents, gang members, judges, community
members, school superintendents, teachers, monks, police, probation officers, correctional staff, lawyers, social services, politicians, ex-cons, nuns, priests, foundation officers, state administrators, and academics have sat together in Circle at Roca. Over
the past seven and a half years, close to one thousand people from
all walks of life have attended the intensive four-day Circle trainings held four or five times a year at Roca. Thousands more have
participated in the Circles held at Roca.

What is it about the Circle that Roca finds so powerful? This is
the key question that we explore in the remaining chapters of this
book. But before we begin that story, it is important to understand
how Roca uses the Circle on a routine and daily basis. According to
records, in a single year, 557 Circles were hosted by Roca. The average number of participants in a Circle was fourteen; some Circles
were as large as seventy participants, while others had as few as six.
Some of the common purposes for sitting in Circle at Roca are

- talking Circles,
- conflict Circles,
- healing Circles,
- family Circles,
- brainstorming and management Circles,
- art Circles,
- court-related Circles,

A Circle of youth at Roca

- visioning Circles, and
- support Circles.

Each Circle shares the basic characteristics of the process: they begin with an opening, come to an agreement on guidelines by exploring shared values, use a talking piece, and close the Circle in good way. The degree of planning, preparation, and follow-up vary depending upon the purpose and intention of the Circle. Often, a Circle that begins for one purpose will serve other purposes as well. All of these Circles are generally described as "peacemaking," because the process builds a foundation of understanding and trust as well as a commitment to shared values that people need to work things out in peaceful ways. As an inherently peace-building process, Circles can be used for many purposes and in all sorts of situations.

Talking Circles are by far the most common type of Circle. These Circles bring people together to share their experiences, thoughts, and beliefs about a particular issue. In 2002, Roca hosted over two hundred talking Circles on various topics. Participants discussed why people join gangs; reasons for leaving school; what it means to be a parent; racism within the community; what it means to participate in civic life; what it takes to go to college; what people leave behind when they emigrate; what it takes to leave gangs; life on the street, and many other issues. As the Circle participants share their experiences, intensely honest discussions ensue about issues that may otherwise be rarely discussed.

Because Circles often bring together people from fundamentally different places in society, these discussions provide powerful opportunities to reduce social distance. The Circle process helps people talk honestly and then listen to experiences different from their own. When people from diverse social backgrounds sit together in Circle, many of the barriers to mutual respect begin to dissolve. The sharing that goes on helps people relate to one another with greater understanding when they are not sitting in Circle.

Padres Unidos, the newcomer-parents group at Roca, organized talking Circles with the superintendent of Chelsea public schools, the director of outreach, the state representative, and the newly appointed principal of Chelsea High School. These newcomer parents had all emigrated to this country within the previous three years from El Salvador, Honduras, Guatemala, Brazil, Argentina, Colombia, and Mexico. The principal was invited to come to a Circle to talk about his vision for the school and to respond to parents' questions and concerns about school policies and academic standards. In turn, the parents used the Circle process to explain why they had made the extremely difficult decision to leave their homes and move to the United States. With deep emotion, they shared with these administrators their heartfelt dreams for the future of their children.

Conflict Circles are held to address difficulties within a particular relationship. For example, they are used to deal with a fight between two youths, tensions between a young person and a parent, or difficulties between two adults. Conflict Circles focus on the relationship between those in conflict by bringing others to the Circle who are affected by that relationship and who can offer perspective and support. On occasion, they may be spontaneous, such as when a flare-up occurs between two youth at Roca. More often, though, conflict Circles are carefully planned events that require deep thought and preparation, so that all those present are ready to be there and are prepared to deal with the underlying conflict.

> "Between a group of young men and another gang, we made an agreement in Circle that when things hit the fan, before they go beating each other up, this person would talk to this one, and that person would talk to that one, to see what the problem is. And we held them accountable for that agreement, and it went well. Four people in this group and four people from that group made the agreement, and they didn't fight each other but held each other accountable, you know, for not making fun of each other, not instigating each other for a good two months after the Circle. Then other things hit the fan, and we had to start over again. But it's an ongoing Circle, and so there was real accountability."
>
> JAMES, ROCA STAFF WORKER

Holding ongoing peacemaking Circles among rival gang members is a prime example of how conflict Circles are used. Sometimes animosity flares between particular individuals; other times it festers between the groups themselves. Conflict Circles focus on transforming the relationship by helping people relate with each other in new ways. Often this means helping them form agreements, such as agreeing not to insult each other or not to hit known trigger points that set off conflicts. Rarely onetime events, conflict Circles usually involve a series of Circles that help the young people take responsibility for resolving or at least managing the conflict. Conflict Circles require a great deal of preparation to build up enough trust for people to attend the Circles, particularly when members from rival gangs are involved.

Support Circles, like those held for Luis before jail, offer encouragement and support to a person undergoing some challenge or deep personal change. Whereas the transformational relationship is primarily one-on-one, the Circle process builds connections among a wider set of people. When a Circle is used for support, it may develop into a visioning process. The Circle creates opportunities for people to articulate their values and vision for themselves and their communities. Like transformational relationships, peacemaking Circles challenge participants to practice being the person they would most like to be. They then offer support to the person as he or she makes life changes that reflect their vision. Support Circles are used to help people go through all kinds of personal transi-
tions. With support, people realize that they are able to imagine a different future and to take concrete steps toward making that vision real for themselves.

Criminologist John Braith-waite envisions using peace-making Circles to give youth

Roca youth

Roca youth

ongoing support. He calls these "youth development Circles." He believes it is important to engage the Circle process as a place for positive growth.[5] Rather than using Circles only as a response to crime or conflicts, Braithwaite proposes making them a permanent feature of a young person's school life. These Circles can focus on a young person's positive development, both educationally and personally. Braithwaite envisions holding a youth development Circle twice a year for young people beginning at age twelve and continuing until he or she makes a successful transition to higher education or a job. This would offer youth the same kind of supportive relationship that Roca practices.

At Roca, the Circle is used for this positive purpose every day. In a sense, it expands the transformational relationship by inviting a wider group of people, including peers, to provide ongoing support for a young person. Beyond the one-on-one relationship, the Circle helps to build a community of care around a young person by bringing all the people who care about him or her together in one room.

The key feature of these communities of care is the unconditional support they offer through a ritual of caring and love. Braithwaite believes that society needs new rituals to re-constitute the "village" needed to raise a child in our urban society. Roca holds that the Circle provides a missing community for people to rally around each other and give the support and encouragement essential to human development. Using Circles on a regular basis does indeed help to build the village that a young person needs to be nurtured in a whole and balanced way.

Healing Circles are another core use of the process. One of the most profound effects of the peacemaking Circle is that it creates space for emotional awareness and healing. In a sense, besides providing a foundation for peace-building, all Circles are also healing Circles. The opportunity to tell one's story in a space where others listen respectfully has enormous potential to salve deep wounds within the community. Because this happens so often in so many Circles, many believe that all Circles involve emotional healing to some degree. Moreover, telling one's story is healing not only for the one who shares but also for those who listen and feel the depths of their own pain resonating with another's story.

The capacity to come together and serve as empathetic witnesses for one another is a powerful source of emotional nourishment. This is particularly true for young people who have experienced considerable trauma and disconnection in their lives. To help young people understand their emotions and control the emotional choices they make in life, Roca has combined the peacemaking Circle with a program on emotional literacy and awareness. "Houses of Healing" is a fourteen-week curriculum originally designed for incarcerated men and women. With Roca's help, this program has been adapted for at-risk youth and is now called "Power Source."[6] By integrating the Power Source curriculum with the Circle process, Roca helps youth deal with the trauma, pain, anger, and loss so common in their daily lives.

Organizational Circles. Finally, Circles are used for organizational purposes, such as management supervision, strategic planning, workshops, and brainstorming. In varying degrees, these Circles combine elements of the Circle process with other meeting formats. The talking piece might be suspended, for example, while participants hear a brief presentation, the Circle keepers open the floor to questions, or a speaker writes on a flip chart. Roca's staff meetings, team meetings, management meetings, and board of directors meetings are all held in Circle. The use of the Circle as an organizational tool has had a transformative impact on Roca and how it interacts with staff members and other community partners.

Opening Doors to Opportunities

Carla is a twenty-one-year-old single mother with two children. Although Carla earned her GED and had solid typing and computer skills, her attitude, dress, and demeanor prevented her from landing a decent job. Paola, a Roca staff person, and Carla had many conversations about this, but still Carla was unwilling to change her behavior. For one job interview, for example, she arrived with her children, having neglected to make arrangements for them in advance. On another occasion, Paola took her shopping to pick out appropriate clothing, but Carla rejected Paola's suggestions, claiming she dressed as "who she was."

When an opportunity opened up at a local bank, Carla decided to apply and, despite doubts that Carla would succeed, Paola agreed to let her try. On the day of the interview, Carla had a painful shock when she arrived at the bank and saw the professional attire of the employees. Humiliated, she fled the interview and disappeared from Roca. In the weeks that followed, Paola pursued her, calling her at home, visiting her, and urging her to learn from this mistake, so that the next time she would be prepared to show up like the professional woman she hoped to become. Gradually, Carla heard what Paola had to say.

Soon a position as a receptionist at a local employment office became available. This time, Carla was ready. She arranged babysitting at Roca for her children and dressed with-

*out an exposed midriff and miniskirt. The interview went well,
and she was offered the job. Shortly afterward, she earned
a promotion and the opportunity to train as a recruiter. Six
months later, she was no longer living at a homeless shelter
and was able to afford a car. Carla continues to meet regularly
with Paola about her career development. In the evenings, she
attends computer classes and brings her children to Roca, so
she can participate in Circles with other young mothers to talk
about their goals and their visions for their futures.*

Roca's first core strategy of streetwork and outreach creates relationships with marginalized youth and draws them into Roca's sphere of activities. Roca's second and third strategies of building transformational relationships and using peacemaking Circles provide the relational scaffolding that young people need to support them in their walk of change. Roca's fourth core strategy makes positive change happen for young people by opening opportunities for a fuller and healthier life.

Once again, this fourth strategy flows from Roca's core values: belonging, generosity, competence, and independence. Through their transformational relationships and participation in peacemaking Circles, the young people at Roca experience a sense of belonging in the world. This is basic. Before young people can forge a positive connection with the world, they must believe that they are loved and belong in it. Their new relationships also cultivate the value of generosity. Each young person begins to realize that he or she has something of value to give to others.

Building a sense of belonging and generosity, however, is not enough. Young adults must earn a living, pay rent, support themselves financially, and, often, support their children as well. Beyond addressing their pressing and immediate needs, young people must also invest in their future through education and career development. Living according to the core values of competence and independence means taking specific actions on the way to building one's life.

Roca defines independence as living out of harm's way and being self-sufficient. Accomplishing this involves a series of achievements that require different levels of competence. Independence includes, for example, making a legitimate income that is sufficient to sustain a dignified lifestyle; having a permanent place to live; forming stable and healthy partnerships; having the capacity to parent children in healthy ways; maintaining one's own physical health; and avoiding harmful behaviors, such as drug abuse, criminal involvement, and violence. Along with these personal goals, Roca adds that competence and independence involve the capacity to envision and lead change for oneself and one's community. The young people learn how to engage fully in the cultural and democratic life of the community, which they will then continue to do throughout their lifetime.

None of this is easy, given a number of economic realities. During our current era, described by some as "late capitalism," many young people find themselves socially excluded from the traditional pathways to stable adult roles within the community.[7] Beginning in the 1970s, employment in manufacturing has declined; jobs have disappeared as technology has improved; and a flight of investment capital out of the United States has caused factories to close. Only the service sector of the economy has grown. These changes have created an increasingly lopsided labor market. On one side are jobs that require lengthy investment in higher education. On the other side are an abundance of ultimately dead-end service-sector jobs that offer little hope for future career development and economic stability.

During this same period, the transition from adolescence to adulthood has become longer, more complex, and less orderly.[8] Developing a stable career and beginning a family occur through graduated steps. To navigate this transition, middle-class youth have routinely relied on their families for financial and emotional support throughout their twenties. This aid from parents ranges from living at home to financial assistance (for education, rent, living expenses, or down payments for a home) to child care. But many other youth lack this enduring support from parents. Foster care children, teen parents, runaways, refugees, immigrant youth, or those with incarcerated parents simply may not receive the emotional and material backing they need to navigate the complex pathways toward stable adult roles.

Furthermore, the young people at Roca often do not qualify for education and employment opportunities. Eligibility requirements, such as age, English-language proficiency, basic literacy, and citizenship status, eliminate them from the running. Moreover, many of Roca's young adults are too old and too far behind—educationally and socially—to benefit from remedial programs. The education options that exist are ill suited to the realities of their lives. As a result, these young people find it exceedingly difficult to take concrete steps toward a stable adulthood.

At age twenty-three, for example, some of the young people who come to Roca may be illiterate or reading at a second-grade level. They may not know how to multiply or divide. Moreover, a host of pressing issues in their lives may make it nearly impossible for them to sit in a classroom or do the work required. Young women with child care responsibilities, for example, cannot bring their children to class or to work, and affordable child care is seldom available. While traveling in certain neighborhoods, active gang members face constant threats to their physical safety. They also have to work around everyday gang-related concerns—safety always being uppermost—that affect their choices of what they can do. Criminal records, frequent periods of incarceration, as well as requirements to show up in court pose more barriers that exclude them from accessing opportunities. Those who struggle with substance abuse issues, mental health limitations, learning disabilities, post-traumatic stress disorder, or trauma from exposure to family or community violence also find themselves excluded from many opportunities.

To build competence and independence, Roca recognizes that it must create opportunities for young people that address all of these obstacles. The young people who are most marginalized require far more than being connected to opportunities in the community. The reason is that, for these individuals, these openings simply do not exist.

As part of this fourth core strategy, Roca offers a wide range of programs that address these issues: ESL (English as Second Language), pre-GED, and GED classes; computer classes; employment readiness and placement training; access to basic health care and family planning; homework support; cultural events; recreation through sports and dance; as well as community-building and civic-participation programs. Just as every program at Roca engages in streetwork and outreach, and each staff person seeks to build transformational relationships with young people and encourages them to sit in Circles, each and every program also offers a range of opportunities to build skills that foster independence.

The combination of these strategies is what makes it all work. Roca's employment program demonstrates the unique synergy of the core strategies. For youth sixteen and older, the route to independence and competence is not primarily through education but through employment. Nationally, almost 5.5 million young adults between the ages of sixteen and twenty-six are both out of school and jobless. Without families to support them, they need jobs to afford a place to live, food, and clothing.

Roca recognizes that pathways to education, health, stable families, and other future goals depend on access to employment. However, most employment programs are either reluctant or unable to serve those who are most at risk, especially young adults. By and large, employment services are not designed to offer the intensive relational support that disconnected young people need to succeed on the job. They need to be taught all kinds of skills that are basic to holding a job, such as punctuality, attendance, how to speak to the boss, what to do when you are going to be late, how to call in sick, how to ask for a raise, and what to wear to an interview.

To open doors to employment, Roca has pioneered a transitional employment model for the most at-risk young people. Instead of offering sixteen weeks of classes that teach employment skills beforehand—e.g., punctuality, attendance, and attitude—Roca's staff members connect a young person with a job as soon as possible. Unlike most employment counselors, a staff member remains in a transformational relationship with the young person while he or she is employed. The combination of direct work experience and intensive interaction with a supportive adult helps the young person learn appropriate work behavior.

> "The TR is the good cop/bad cop balance, but there are very clear goals young people need in order to succeed in the world. They need to not have bad attitudes, they need to watch their language, they need to show up at work, they need to not be lazy. Okay, you're in a bad mood? You still gotta show up to work. You're sick? You still gotta show up to work. You had a bad day? You still gotta show up. Every time you are in a bad mood, I can't stop the world for you. And I'm not going to, 'cause nobody else will."
>
> SUSAN, ROCA STAFF

When the young people make mistakes, as Carla did, or get fired from a job for poor performance, as often happens, Roca does not react by excluding the youth from the program or by labeling them as failures. Mistakes present valuable learning opportunities. Attaching young people to an opportunity, such as a job, is not an end but a means to further a young person's growth and development. When Carla finally landed the job of her dreams, her continued involvement with Roca—especially through the transformational relationships and the Circles—helped her envision for herself an even better job. She stayed focused step by step on her journey toward a healthy adulthood.

Working with Other Institutions for Systemic Change

"Abandoned youth" do not appear out of nowhere. Their existence is created by the policies and practices of our societal institutions, which all too often exacerbate situations for youth who are already in crisis. "Street-involved" youth are invariably "system-involved." The personnel of law enforcement, the courts, social services, and correctional agencies are the primary adults who respond when young people become disconnected from safe or stable homes. Families too often abandon their unruly youth to the social services or criminal justice system. "In this state," observes the area director of the Department of Social Services, "you can dispose of your child easier than you can get rid of the old tires on your car." By filing a CHINS (Child in Need of Services) petition with the court, overburdened families routinely ask the state to take over the supervision and care of their youth.

The core institutions charged with dealing with young people who are disconnected from families and schools, by and large, treat young people as "problems" that must be segregated, fixed, or punished. The institutional attitude toward young people is "follow the rules or else,"—"or else" being the threat of their eventual exclusion from a youth facility. All too often, this response escalates over time to more or less permanent removal from society through incarceration.

In line with this thinking, zero-tolerance policies have become common strategies for dealing with disruptive youth, whether in schools, shopping malls, or other institutions. For example, in order to preserve safety and order on school property, schools set stringent attendance requirements, weapons policies, rules against fighting, and penalties for tardiness. Violating these rules pushes young people out of school. With their parents either absent or working full-time, youth are left to roam the community without adult guidance. Excluded from the institutions charged with supervising young people in this society, these "throw-away" youth claim leftover spaces in empty parking lots and vacant buildings. Yet the more time they spend on the street, the more likely they are to come under the "supervision" of the criminal justice system.

> "We deal with the ones who have been kicked out of everywhere else. They've been kicked out of the traditional youth programs and other places; they've been kicked out of school; they've been kicked out of their house. Where do people think they go? They are still here. They are a part of our community."
>
> MOLLY, ROCA'S EXECUTIVE DIRECTOR

Roca has long understood that, to support youth, it must work closely with all the adults and agencies responsible for them within the community. On a daily basis, staff members are in contact with personnel from schools, the police, mental health agencies, health clinics, social services, juvenile services, courts, and city officials. Over the years, there has been no shortage of meetings, phone calls, reports, memos, discussions, coalitions, and task forces to respond to the needs of youth. Yet despite hard work and good intentions, collaborative partnerships have often failed to evolve from these interactions. At times, misunderstanding and distrust among the adults have even increased the obstacles for struggling youth.

> "I remember the night I realized things had to change. There had been violence on the street, and we were

concerned about the safety of a particular young man. So I marched up to the Chelsea police station and went head to head, chest to chest with the lieutenant on duty, demanding that he listen to us. I was not exactly the image of a peacemaker at that moment, and we did not have the best communication. As I left the police station, it suddenly hit me that I had probably just made the world less safe for that young person that night, which was the very opposite of what I was trying to do."

MOLLY, ROCA'S EXECUTIVE DIRECTOR

In 1999, Roca began to collaborate with community partners in a fundamentally different way. This shift came as a direct result of Roca's decision to adopt peacemaking Circles as a core strategy. Roca had tried to build relationships with other agencies and institutions for many years. The Circle process finally gave Roca an alternative method for doing this, a method that cultivates trust, mutual understanding, respect, and a deeper relationship between individuals. By practicing Circles, Roca made the shift from an adversarial style of working with other youth organizations and institutions to an approach based on respect, inclusiveness, and tolerance.

"Three years later at a hearing on a proposed gang ordinance, the chief of police stood up and explained to the city council why having his officers go out and just arrest kids would not solve the gang problem and might even make matters worse. The answer, he told the city council, was for his officers to work with places like Roca. Three years earlier, that never would have happened. Because we had learned how to show up in a different way, we made space for others to change too."

MOLLY, ROCA'S EXECUTIVE DIRECTOR

It's All about Change

Of necessity, Roca is committed to understanding how individuals, families, communities, and organizations change. Every strategy that Roca uses is designed to promote or support positive change in the lives of young people. According to the model that Roca has developed, change begins with relationships. When an adult interacts with a young person whose life has been mostly on the street, the youth is taking his or her first step toward transformation. The all-important streetwork involves showing up for marginalized young people unconditionally and with respect. Even though a young person may be doing harm to others and himself or herself, Roca nonetheless sees that youth as more than just a problem that must somehow be made to go away.

From the start, then, the relationship is guided by a set of values that asserts, "This person is a precious human being who has much to give." The transformational relationship that develops endures all kinds of upheavals and persists in promoting positive change over time. Through ups and downs—"three steps forward and two steps back"—the adult stays committed to the young person's growth and development. The relationship becomes a solid connection that the young person can count on.

Peacemaking Circles build a different kind of relationship among a wider group of people, yet these relationships are built on the same values and commitment as the transformational relationship. The Circle's power lies in its ability to promote a different way for us to be in relationship with each other. The Circle also opens a space for collective visioning, which is essential for developing new patterns of relationships within society.

Roca's strategic methods—streetwork, transformational relationships, and peacemaking Circles—differ radically from the customary model of relationships in modern society. In fact, many people find it hard to practice this alternative and "new" approach to relationships, because these are the very methods we

Roca youth

are taught to set aside whenever we go outside the family. We generally espouse values of unconditional acceptance, respect, mutual understanding, and love with family members and perhaps intimate friends. However, we are neither expected nor taught to practice these values with strangers, much less in the competitive worlds of the workplace, political life, or marketplace.

What is so radical about Roca's approach is its commitment to building relationships based on these values not only with young people but also—and just as critically—with other adults in the community. No matter what the relationship, the purpose is transformation, and the method is changing *how* we relate with one another. A transformational relationship urges us to keep asking ourselves: Which values are we bringing to this relationship?

Roca arrived at this approach for practical reasons based on decades of experience. The mission to create places that invite change cannot be simply about young people and their families. For the lives of young people to change, patterns within the community and larger society must change too. Youth at the margin are not the only ones who must undergo transformation: the adults at the center—those who hold positions of power and authority—must change as well.

Roca's work with other institutions is, therefore, about supporting systemic change. Roca uses the same strategic methods in its work with schools, courts, juvenile authorities, governments, religious institutions, and businesses that it uses with disconnected young people. That is, being in relationships that are guided by values forms the foundation for profound change. So, whether a young person struggles to leave a gang or a department of social services struggles to develop its organization to better meet the needs within the community, the demands of change are similar.

And change is demanding. Change is, as we know, a non-linear process. It has ups and downs—not only forward steps but also sideways and backwards ones. To make it through this process, people need consistent support in creating a vision of what they want and who they want to be and then in taking concrete steps toward making their vision a reality.

Moreover, change does not occur all at once. It happens through incremental shifts in habits. Individuals and groups are generally motivated to change when they experience a creative tension between how things are and how they could be. The "how things are" side of this tension requires an honest and often painful awareness of the "truth" of what is really going on. The "how things could be" calls for an aspiration or vision—a willingness to imagine what might not have seemed possible before. Creating an environment where people can both confront hard realities and imagine themselves and the world differently is one of the core goals of transformational relationships and peacemaking Circles.

Because of this creative tension, making positive change tends to be uncomfortable. When people start to shift out of their "comfort zones," they gradually abandon one set of habits—attitudes, feelings, and behaviors—and replace them with a different set of behaviors, attitudes, and feelings. As people act differently, they need support, guidance, recognition, encouragement, and help from others.

Relationships, then, provide the scaffolding for all the change processes that Roca seeks for young people. Clearly, change is more than an internal or individual process; it's something fundamentally relational. Yet not just any kind of relationship supports change. Roca has developed a sophisticated method for building the kinds of relationships that promote positive development in those who are struggling to grow and change their lives.

CHAPTER FOUR

The Circle as a Space of Empowerment

It is now time to tell the story of Circles at Roca. In a complex world of advanced science, digital interconnections, genetic engineering, global transport, and high-speed communication, why would we want to learn something that in our culture is most commonly practiced among our youngest children? What is the power hidden within such a humble process?

The Circle is neither a panacea nor a magic wand that makes social problems suddenly disappear. It is more like a form of social technology that enables us to tap capacities for wisdom, collective support, and creativity that lie dormant within us. By engaging the Circle process, we learn how to create a sacred space. In this space, we are able to lift barriers between us and open ourselves to fresh possibilities for connection, collaboration, creativity, and mutual understanding.

To go deeper into the effect that Circles can have, we may well consider what might be missing from our current relationships—with ourselves as well as within our families, communities, and institutions—that the Circle helps us rediscover and reclaim. Somehow this space gently liberates a truth that many people have locked away in their hearts: we all want to love and be loved.

> "Everybody sits in a Circle, and regardless of where they're from, whatever culture or background, regardless of that, the reason we are all there is because

we understand that we just want love, we just want
peace. And I just think that it is so beautiful."

A SEVENTEEN-YEAR-OLD YOUNG WOMAN AT ROCA

What Is the Peacemaking Circle, Really?

The actual Circle process is akin to the tip of the iceberg: the real
force comes from the values that the Circle embodies. These values
lay beneath the surface and are practiced through the structure
and rituals of the Circle itself. Ritual and ceremony are nonverbal,
almost unconscious forms of collective communication through
which we develop and affirm shared understandings.

Most of the rituals we unconsciously participate in every day
are rituals of power. They reinforce hierarchies of control and continually remind us of our "place" in systems of inequality. Think
of the traditional classroom with its podium of authority: all eyes
stay focused on the teacher who holds the sacred power of speech.
Or consider the ritual of the courtroom: the judge is clothed in
black robes and elevated above everyone else. The judge interacts only with lawyers and their clients, all of whom are separated
from people in the community by a bar or railing. The ritual of
an intake assessment when a social worker makes an official assessment of a family's situation carries a similar message. The
professional person demands that families disclose intimate details to total strangers, who remain mute even about insignificant
aspects of their own lives.

A ritual is not a passive experience. When we perform rituals,
we are *doing* the structure of society, literally *acting out* the structure of our relationships with one another. So, too, when we sit in
Circle, we are practicing relationships, but of a different kind. The
rituals of the Circle affirm a social order based on inclusiveness,
equality, and respect for all participants. In Circles, everyone is
an equal part of the whole; there is no "head" and no hierarchy.
Regardless of age or status, each person has his or her own indi-

A Circle of youth at Roca

vidual place, and there is no place outside the Circle. Generally, Circles have no observers: everyone who is present becomes part of the Circle.

As a result, there is no "table" to hide behind or back of the room to retreat to. Each person faces the others as a human being, leaving titles that signify position or rank behind and using first names only. Everyone is given an equal chance to participate and is encouraged to speak from their hearts and from their own experiences. In these ways, the rituals of the Circles offer a way to "act out" a very different kind of social structure.

Those who suffer under the rituals of hierarchy—as young people routinely do—appreciate the structure of the Circle, precisely because of its practice of an egalitarian worldview. Every place is equal; every voice is valued. Whatever the issue, many different perspectives are needed to fully understand what is going on. Coming together in the Circle, the participants make up a continuous whole and become a force for transformation that is far greater than the mere sum of the individuals acting separately.

The Circle process reflects deep wisdom about human nature and life. Through its egalitarian structure, the Circle honors the principles of the Medicine Wheel. These cycles are typically described as fourfold processes: the four stages of life—infancy, adolescence, adulthood, and old age; the four seasons of the year; the four elements of wind, fire, rain and earth; and the four dimensions of human beings—physical, mental, emotional, and spiritual. Though distinct, each phase or aspect is an integral part of a larger whole. Each element forms an essential part of our natural existence and is held in balance around a sacred center, a central fire. Differences are held equally in balance.

According to this worldview, when people cause harm either to others or to themselves, they are living out of balance in some way. And if one person is out of balance, then the larger community is out of balance as well, since all life—all of us—are interconnected. The path toward a solution begins with understanding the problem in all its relatedness. By listening to what each person brings to the Circle, we begin to discover what needs to shift, so that everyone involved moves toward balance.

Not only the Circle's structure but also its rhythm reflects the wisdom of the Medicine Wheel. Circles include four interdependent and continuous phases that are marked by ceremonies. First, Circles begin with an opening and introductions. Second, Circles include time for checking in and making connections. Third, Circles spend time identifying issues and seeking solutions. Finally, Circles make time to close in a good way.

In the dominant culture, we tend to focus on problems immediately. This "rush-to-fix" approach emphasizes what is going wrong rather than what is going right; it is deficit-based rather than asset-based. By contrast, the rituals of the Circle set a pace that helps participants identify their strengths as individuals and as a community before they begin to address their weaknesses.

The wisdom of the Medicine Wheel built into the Circle process teaches people to take the time to build connections, even in small ways, before beginning the hard work of facing the sources of separation.

Acknowledging the wisdom embedded in the overall ritual of the Circle, many people experience it as "a gift from the Creator." The Circle is, indeed, a harmonious method for bringing people together "in a good way." It helps us understand the dynamics among us and make decisions that honor the relatedness inherent in every situation. A balanced, harmonious process is the best way to restore balance and harmony to a world torn by divisions.

The Hidden Lessons of Circle

Early one morning, one of Roca's mentors, Harold Gatensby of the T'lingit First Nation in Yukon, slipped into the room where the chairs had been carefully set up for a morning Circle. When the staff and young people entered the room, instead of the familiar arrangement of a Circle of chairs facing a center, they found four rows of chairs at right angles forming a square. With a sly grin, Harold leaned back in his chair and turned to the group: "So what are we going to do now? Do you think it's time for me to teach you about the square? Can we have a Circle if we are sitting in a square?"

How easy it is to confuse the outer form for the thing itself! By putting the chairs into a square, Harold was reminding Roca to pay attention to the underlying meaning of the Circle and not to be distracted by its outer shape. The nuts and bolts of the Circle process are important only because they help us learn how to "sit in Circle with each other." This has very little to do with the furniture arrangement. Using a talking piece; opening and closing mindfully; agreeing on guidelines; facing one another across a glowing candle; even sitting in a circle: all of these practices help

Roca youth

us be in a good way with ourselves and others. They are ancient and wise methods that gently remind our all-too-human selves of certain important values. The form is not the thing itself: to sit in Circle, we don't need to be sitting in a circle.

The Seven (Hidden) Lessons of the Circle

At the end of their second year of learning about the Circle, Roca staff members were ready to reflect on what they were beginning to understand about the process. Some of the lessons that emerged highlight the underlying meanings that Harold had been teaching them.

1. "A way to be." The first lesson is that the Circle is not a technique or a program but a way to be. The Circle is a commitment to practice living the values of the Circle. The more people sit in Circle at Roca, the more they realize that the Circle is not about sitting in the physical space but about learning how to be in Circle when you are not sitting in Circle. The meaning of "being in Circle" has expanded to refer to acting in a "Circle way" or holding oneself "in a good way" in one's relationships with one's self and others.

2. *A sacred space.* The second lesson is that the Circle is a sacred space unlike many others. Opening and closing in a good way and using rituals and ceremony—such as burning sage, playing music, or setting up a meaningful centerpiece—are all elements that preserve the Circle as a place that is cherished and honored. Participants must be intentional and purposeful about maintaining the sacredness of the space.

3. *Personal sharing.* The third lesson is that Circles are about giving oneself up to the Circle experience by sharing our personal stories to help others. At Roca, two core values are generosity and belonging. The Circle incorporates both these values. In the Circle, everyone has a place; everyone belongs. On this basis, the Circle becomes a space that invites participants to share their stories. This is an extraordinary gift to others. Opening our experiences to the Circle is an act of generosity that reinforces belonging: people feel less alone when they know the experiences of others. The lessons of modeling Circle values and giving oneself up to the Circle are some of the more personally challenging aspects of engaging with the Circle process. Yet, they are also essential to making the Circle most effective in spurring transformation.

4. *Mutual accountability.* The fourth lesson is that Circles foster accountability to one's self and others. In the Circle, participants are invited to meet their own hopes for themselves. Who do they really want to be? The Circle guidelines that participants work out together and agree upon are themselves a deep lesson in accountability. Only when people hold themselves accountable to acting in accordance with the guidelines will the Circle be a space that is respectful, caring, honest, and so forth. This lesson extends to holding ourselves accountable for actions outside of Circle. Learning to be "in a good way" with oneself and others both inside and outside the Circle is a critical lesson that emerges from being in Circle.

5. *"Trusting the process."* The truth that no one controls the Circle is lesson number five. Circles are spaces of collective empowerment and leadership. The phrases "letting go" and "trust the process" are often used to describe the need to relinquish expectations and a desire to control the outcome. The Circle takes on a life of its own, and learning to be a servant of that process is one of the challenges of being a keeper. Sitting in Circle often demonstrates the wisdom that everyone brings gifts and that true power comes from the group rather than a leader.

6. *Participation is voluntary.* Lesson number six is that no one can be forced to sit in Circle. Roca soon realized that making youth sit in Circle doesn't work; it goes against Circle values. Instead, Roca continually invites young people to come to the Circle and prepares them to do so without relying upon traditional forms of threats, coercion, or pressure. Because the transformational model of change is so fundamental at Roca, staff members recognize the importance of keeping the invitation open. They realize that young people need support as they take incremental steps out of their comfort zones. Circles call for the same attitude of patient persistence. Keeping the invitation open without pressuring people to be in Circle has been a significant learning experience for Roca.

7. *"It's about us."* Lesson number seven is that the Circle is not about the Circle; it's about us. This insight comes back to the first lesson: the Circle is not a thing or a program but a way to be. The awesome power of the Circle is not the magic of a ritual or technique but the enormous capacity of people to heal and solve problems when they come together in a good way. Creating that space, whether it is a Circle or not, is what matters. The Circle is one way—but not necessarily the only way—to access what lies untapped within the community, namely, the ability to come together in a loving way for ourselves and for our future.

The Rituals of the Circle

Again, rituals are intentional processes for acting out relationships based on a particular worldview and set of values. The ritual of the Circle includes a number of specific practices that draw on the values and worldview underlying Circles.

Openings and closings. The purpose of an opening is to mark the Circle gathering as different from an ordinary meeting. An opening might be a poem, quotation, music, meditation, or minute of silence. Almost anything can serve as an opening. The ritual helps people transition into a different kind of space and promotes a certain attitude toward that space. The same is done at the end of the Circle with a brief reading or an expression of a heartfelt wish. The opening sets the tone and the closing reminds participants of positive values, of hope, of progress they may have made, and of the commitment they bring to the Circle. As bad as the problem may be and as difficult as the conversation is, the purpose is to seek a better future. Openings and closings help participants stay focused on their capacities to create a better future.

> "Roca has learned that openings are only openings when they feel welcoming to the people in the Circle. In the multicultural world of Roca, what is welcoming to some may be threatening to others. In one Circle, for example, a number of young men who had recently arrived in the United States from Sudan balked at the lighting of sage for the opening ritual. Having fled a region where religious conflict led to terrible violence, these young men feared any connection to any particular religion in their new home and immediately got up and left the room."
>
> VICTOR, ROCA STAFF

The importance of opening and closing "in a good way" reflects the wisdom that it is not possible to achieve a good outcome through a process that does not model what you hope to achieve. Chief Justice Robert Yazzie expresses this insight quite simply by saying, "You cannot get to a good place in a bad way."[1] A process aimed at improving the lives of people struggling with hurt and conflict must model the practice of being in a good way with one another.

The talking piece. One of the most transformative elements of the Circle is the use of a talking piece. In Native communities, the talking piece is traditionally an eagle feather, but it can also be a rock, a stick, or any object that has meaning to the community convening the Circle. Only the person holding the talking piece may speak, and any participant is free to pass the talking piece without speaking. The talking piece generally moves around the Circle in a clockwise direction following the path of the sun.

Discussing values and agreeing on guidelines. At the start of every Circle, participants spend time discussing how they wish to treat one another within the Circle and what each participant needs in order to feel "safe." This is the ritual of exploring values and setting guidelines based on them. People generally articulate values such as respect, trust, honesty, confidentiality, and patience. The process can take a long time, as people grapple with what the values really mean, the implications of living them, and whether or not they can agree to practice them in the Circle. This may be the first time many people, especially young people, may have articulated their values. It gives them a chance to reflect on what their experiences have been around a particular value and the value's significance in their lives.

Creating consensus. Agreeing on guidelines requires consensus. Even before tackling the "problem" that brought people to a Circle, participants practice coming to an agreement when they discuss values and then agree on guidelines. Unlike rules that are invented and enforced by someone in a position of authority, guidelines reflect how the group decides collectively to be with one another. Once again, the ritual of agreeing on guidelines carries a deeper lesson. Whereas in most social contexts, a structure of authority enforces compliance with rules, the Circle creates a place of shared leadership. Coming to agreement on the guidelines carries the profound lesson that the values are meaningless unless each participant is committed to practicing them.

The role of keepers. Every Circle has at least one and often two "keepers." Keepers are facilitators. They are responsible for "holding the space" of the Circle. The responsibilities of the keeper include: assisting people in getting ready for the Circle; planning the Circle; arranging the physical space; preparing an opening, a closing, and a set of questions; welcoming people; and maintaining the rituals and tone during the Circle. During the Circle itself, the keeper poses questions and topics, passes the talking piece, clarifies issues, sometimes takes notes, and records agreements. Keepers will make many decisions during a Circle, such as when to keep the talking piece circulating; when to take a break or switch to a new topic; and when it is time to close a Circle and plan for another.

The keeper is not, however, responsible for the outcome of the Circle. The keeper's role is distinct from the Western role of a mediator. Keepers are not professionals but people familiar with the Circle process and its underlying values. Young people, parents, or community members may serve as keepers of the Circle. It is not the job of the keeper to bring people to agreement or to find a solution. Keeping is a skill that involves maintaining an atmosphere of respect and safety. Keepers neither control the process nor are responsible for its outcome.

"Trusting the Circle." In many Indigenous cultures, genuine leadership is understood to be situational. That is, for every challenge, a person will emerge who is uniquely situated to provide

Roca youth

the inspiration and wisdom needed at that moment. In a family Circle, it may be a young person, an aunt, or a neighbor who shares just the right memory, funny joke, or heartfelt insight that helps people move beyond a particular stalemate or conflict. The structure of the Circle allows the creativity and leadership within each person to come forward. Because it is impossible to know beforehand who will emerge as a leader within the Circle, experienced keepers often say that they trust the Circle to handle the situation when it becomes difficult or tense. Of course, they trust not the Circle per se but the wisdom and creativity of those engaged in the Circle to find a way toward a constructive solution.

The Power of Being Seen and Heard

Roca set out to create a place where all young people belong, because they realized that a basic sense of connection was missing in the lives of many young people. Young people need a concrete sense that they belong in the world and that they are valued as contributing members of a community. Without this, they are unlikely to develop the habits of responsibility, perseverance, self-discipline, and self-care that are necessary to carry them through the many steps toward a stable adulthood.

The Circle promotes a sense of belonging and helps young people become aware of their own purpose and value to others. The Circle does this by opening up a space where all people are truly "seen" and "heard." The extent to which young people in our society feel excluded and invisible is most evident by the difference it makes when they are truly recognized and heard by others.

The Invisibility of Youth

> "For kids from the street, not too many people stop and ask, 'How you doing?' Circles help to do that. For once in their lifetime, they sit in a Circle and there's a check in: 'How you doing?' 'How you feeling?' Young people got so much to say, but they've been neglected for so many years—just left out on the street. People don't understand them, parents don't understand them, and they're just left out there. They want to talk to people, and they want to share their stuff, but they don't know how to do it in a good way, and that's what Circles do."
>
> VICHEY, ROCA STAFF

Among the Zulu in South Africa, a common greeting is the word 'Sawubona.' It roughly translates as "Hello," but it actually means something quite different. When the Zulu use this word, they are saying "I see you"—not your clothes, your position, the way your hair is done, if you are rich, young, poor, or old. What this greeting means is: "I acknowledge your presence, because I see the unique spirit that is you, and by acknowledging you, I bring you into existence, just as your acknowledgment of me brings me into existence." The Zulu believe we exist as unique and valued people insofar as we "see each other" in community. For the Zulu, the failure to acknowledge other people is to literally threaten their existence.

In Western society, we tend to "see" the positions that people occupy or the roles they perform within society. We see Mrs. Smith the mother, Frank the police officer, Mrs. Jones the executive director, or Mr. Hingham the teacher. The higher one's status in the hierarchy of positions, the more this person is "heard" and acknowledged in the context of that role.

Lacking formal positions, young people are rarely heard by adults. In school, young people occupy the voiceless bottom of a hierarchy where they are most often treated as objects of adult manipulation and control. Beyond the early grades, a typical classroom is not organized to appreciate the unique value of each child. Schools generally acknowledge children on the basis of their academic achievements: young people who do not succeed are defined by their failures.

Within the family, adults are often unwilling or unable to truly acknowledge a young person or listen to what he or she has to say. Some cultural traditions neither expect nor invite young people to be heard by adults. Within many homes, adults are absent, overworked, or lost to addiction or illness. As a result, they are psychologically incapable of providing this kind of acknowledgment. The ceaseless blare of the television or other electronic entertainment displaces real communication among family members.

Before long, the wider culture comes to view nonconforming young people not as unique and precious souls to be cherished but as troublesome "populations" to be suppressed, controlled, forcibly removed, or even eliminated. They are kicked out of their homes or schools, as if they somehow vanish into thin air when they are excluded. Persistent, these young people push hard to be seen in this world, whether by joining gangs, writing graffiti, doing crime, or engaging in violence. They soon become young mothers and fathers in an attempt to create relationships where they will be seen as a significant, important presence in the eyes of another human being.

> "A lot of these young people are in such a state that they don't respect themselves. They don't acknowledge any good part about themselves, and they feel, 'I don't belong here; I don't belong anywhere.' So the first step is really to say: 'You belong in this world.'"
>
> SUSAN, ROCA STAFF

The experience of belonging at Roca is fundamentally about being seen and treated as a person of value. When young people come into the building, someone is always there to notice them. Someone greets them by name, asks about their day, remembers when they were last there and what they did, and knows what they like, who their friends are, where they live, and with whom they live. Transformational relationships are an intentional effort to see each young person for all his or her singularity, talent, and beauty. They are about paying attention to young people— and not only for things they have done wrong or because of their deficits and problems.

Adults talk a great deal about developing the voice of young people and about promoting their participation in democracy or civic affairs. But the development of voice is not only about young people. "Voice" is a collaborative achievement: it involves both the willingness of the speaker to talk and the willingness of an audience to be attentive. For young people to be seen and heard, adults must see and listen. As clinical psychologist Kaethe Weingarten puts it, "Voice depends on witnessing."[2]

The Circle opens a place where this happens: the unique presence of each person is seen and brought to life through others' acknowledgment of them. This is obvious in the Circle's physical structure: no one is outside the Circle; everyone is included and belongs. Creating an opportunity for people to be heard respectfully and fully is one of the most meaningful elements of the Circle process. By using the talking piece and being guided by the values of the Circle, participants create an environment where they can speak and be heard—a powerful experience for those who are routinely silenced in our society. The Circle process opens a space of Sawubona where all people—young and old—are "seen."

The Transformative Power of the Talking Piece

> *Few environments are more controlled than a secure juvenile detention facility. The first time the director of a detention center decided to try a Circle with thirty young women in the locked facility, she warned the visitors from Roca, "Don't expect too much." Yet the unexpected happened. "I've got girls with mental health issues in here, and some young women who are testing all the time. Usually they all talk at once; even kids who are very cooperative blurt things out. But that didn't happen during the Circle, not once. There was complete respect for the talking piece, and this was the first Circle! I was amazed. I could not believe it. None of them violated the talking piece! No one! They totally respected the Circle. And they loved it. The first thing they asked when it was over was, 'When are we gonna do that again?'"*

It is not surprising that young people find the ritual of using the talking piece so liberating, because it levels the structure of relationships from hierarchy to equality. With the talking piece, the Circle offers everyone an opportunity to share and be empowered. The leveling power of the talking piece opens up a space where young people can participate fully and equally. Young people are instantly attracted to places where they are treated as equals.

"There is a very big difference between being told you
are equal and feeling and seeing that you are equal. The
Circle looks and feels like a place of genuine equality."

MOLLY, ROCA'S EXECUTIVE DIRECTOR

The power of the talking piece to transform the way we speak
to one another reveals how rarely we make connection through
language. Speaking in a meeting, classroom, or family encounter
is more often a contest of status and power rather than a communication that creates trust and connection. The Circle process offers a singular opportunity for people to communicate as equals.
Everyone in the Circle, including the keeper, is afforded the same
privilege: "Speak all you wish when you hold the talking piece."
You may pass, but as long as you hold the piece, others will respectfully listen. When you are finished speaking, you pass it to
the person to your left.

With the talking piece, each person may talk without fear of
being interrupted or disrespected by distracting side conversations. The Circle protects each speaker from the dynamics of
domination. The rules are simple and obvious, but the outcome
is powerful. Those who are routinely silenced are empowered,
while those who are accustomed to monopolizing conversations
are gently disempowered. A principal at a local high school was
invited to a Circle at Roca to explore why young people drop out
of school. It was clear from the outset that the Circle did not allow him to interact with students and parents in his customary
manner.

About thirty-five people attended a Circle at Roca to discuss
why young people were dropping out of school. Participants
in the Circle included the superintendent of schools, the high
school principal, Cambodian and Latino parents, Roca staff,
young people who had dropped out, and young people who
were still in school. The principal had never participated in a

Circle before. As the talking piece slowly made its way around the Circle, he became increasingly agitated. Unable to ask questions or to respond to people as they spoke, he began to fidget, crossing and uncrossing his legs, sitting on the edge of his chair, as the feather neared his seat.

When he finally took hold of the talking piece, his face colored as he expressed his intense frustration with the ritual of the talking piece. He complained that it was inefficient, because he had forgotten points he wanted to make in response to comments made earlier. He explained that he had had questions that he wanted to ask after someone spoke and rejoinders he needed to make, but now it was too late; the moment has passed. . . .

The Circle respectfully listened. As he trailed off, the principal asked the keepers if he could use his turn to pose questions to specific people in the Circle and hand the feather to them for their response. The keeper simply reminded him of the ritual: speak while he held the piece, and pass it to the person sitting on his left when he was done. If others chose to, they would respond to his questions when the feather came to them. He shook his head and abruptly passed the feather.

As the feather moved around the Circle, several young people responded with sympathy to the principal's anxiety about the Circle. They, too, had anxieties when they first sat in Circle and suggested he might jot down notes, as they sometimes did, so as not to forget what he wanted to say. One young person shared the revelation that when he forgot something he wanted to say, he often realized it wasn't all that important in the first place. Another young person said she found that others often made the point she wanted to make, so it wasn't necessary for her to worry about getting the feather to share her idea. The point that came to her had already been put into the Circle by someone else. In a pro-

found reversal of roles, the young people offered wisdom and advice to the all-powerful adult.

The principal's frustration with the Circle was not really about his loss of memory. He was really objecting to his loss of privilege in the conversation. Like other adults in positions of authority, the principal was adept at using language to frame issues, make points, extract answers, and shape the discussion with subordinates. The cross-examination style of interrogation is designed to manipulate the words of a "hostile witness" in a battle between two opposing versions of truth. The interrogator puts words into the mouth of the witness, demanding that he or she accept or reject a particular version of reality.

The strategy—designed to establish the supremacy of one view and discredit all others—makes no allowance for the "gray." It rejects the idea that reality is multifaceted and that there may be many sides to a truthful understanding of an issue. The interrogation strategy uses speech to push an agenda, cajole, or persuade others to agree with one position. It is not about seeking a more complete understanding of another person's perspective or exploring his or her concerns about an issue. In this culture, speech is often used to intimidate, interrogate, control, demand, ridicule, or manipulate in order to show that we are right and others are wrong.

Much to his chagrin, the principal discovered that the ritual of the talking piece robbed him of his ability to use language to direct the thoughts and actions of others. Barry Stuart points out that the Circle "shuts up" the people who are paid to talk. Lawyers, teachers, principals, politicians, and executives are trained to use language as a tool of power. Professionals are often paid to speak on behalf of those who are less powerful and choose words that will represent someone else's experiences and interests. Yet rarely do professionals listen to ordinary people when they tell their own stories and share their experiences in their own time and in their own ways. Rarely do powerful adults listen to the advice, stories, opinions, anecdotes, and wisdom of youth or less powerful adults, such as poor immigrant parents.

Despite his discomfort and much to his credit, the principal agreed to continue attending a series of talking Circles with parents and students about school issues. In these Circles, participants—including parents, administrators, teachers, current students, and dropouts—shared stories from their own experiences. They talked about what had helped them when they were struggling to succeed in school or during other key challenges in their lives. Students talked about how they felt at school, whether they felt supported, and with whom they felt a connection and why. Although the principal still found the Circle frustrating, he discovered a different kind of power in Circle: the power of listening.

> "In the Circle, students expressed to the principal that they understood that he really cared about them, but they felt he didn't show it in his behavior at school. I've sat in on many conversations between school administrators and young people or parents, and often I find administrators to be really dismissive of what is being said. You know, like, that doesn't really happen, or it used to happen but not anymore. This time was different. After the Circle, the very next day at announcements, the principal went on for maybe five or ten minutes about how great the kids are. He later said that being in Circle really changed his way of being a principal."
>
> JESSICA, ROCA STAFF WORKER

In reality, the talking piece is more about listening than it is about talking. The power of the ritual lies in the space it creates for listening. Most of the time that people spend in Circles is indeed spent listening rather than speaking. Using a talking piece helps people pay attention to what is actually being said, because they're not distracted by thoughts about breaking in or how to respond. Participants learn patience as the talking piece moves around the Circle. The pace slows down and becomes more reflective, as people concentrate on what others are saying. People have more time to think before responding. An environment for listening is created that exists in few other places in our culture.

Roca youth

Honoring the Invitation

"Once young people are allowed to be themselves, they grow. They do it themselves. If we keep getting in their way, they'll grow the less for it. The language around here is: 'We need to put them in Circle'; 'They need Circle'; 'This person needs to sit in Circle.' Yet who are we to tell somebody else what they need? So it's really how we hold ourselves in a place where we allow them to be themselves in this world in a way that doesn't make them look like there's always something wrong with them."

SAYRA, ROCA STAFF

Using Circles only as a response to some young person's bad behavior or to a conflict or problem reinforces disempowering patterns and negative stereotypes about young people. Especially in our work with youth and communities, the habit is to focus on the negative instead of the positive. During the first year of Circle learning at Roca, staff members felt pressured to sit young people down in Circle. They sought leverage to get the young people to come to Circles. Yet requiring young people to sit in a Circle or viewing Circles as a response to trouble or problems undermines the nature of the Circle as a place for genuine empowerment. Viewing Circles as an exclusively problem-centered process prevents young people and the community from using them in self-directed and empowering ways.

Promoting participation in Circles in ways that are more closely aligned with the Circle's philosophy and values, then, means finding ways to invite young people to a Circle without relying on various forms of coercion—punishments or rewards. To be a space for genuine equality, the Circle process must be genuinely voluntary. Young people must be able to choose freely whether or not they want to participate. They will not feel good about being in Circle if adults ask them to come only when there is a problem or conflict. Neither is the Circle a space where young people should be "sat," since the choice to be in Circle is important for young people to make for themselves. Being able to say no to a Circle is essential to the Circle's overall effectiveness and integrity as a process.

Yet even when young people say no, the invitation remains open. Granted, carrying out this policy is easier said than done, since young people—indeed, all people—sometimes need help in making healthy decisions. Yet one of the Circle's lessons is that "holding the space" requires patience. Keeping the invitation open to Circle requires persistence, tolerance, and love. When young people trust the invitation—trust that it is not another form of coercion by adults, trust that Circles are what people say they are—then they will come of their own accord and with commitment.

Empowering the Voice of Youth through Circles

"I pretty much can't talk in front of people, so the Circle gives me confidence and makes me feel com-

fortable about myself to just be myself and just talk.
That's what I like about it most. The Circle gives me
that safe zone to open up and talk. People are there
to listen. I can express myself and talk about whatever the Circle is focused on. . . . In the Circle, I feel
secure. People get to express whatever people got to
say; they have a voice. At a meeting, people just sort
of lash out and say whatever they want, and some
people don't have the same amount of talking time or
express the same amount."

VICHEY, ROCA STAFF

"When we don't use Circles, I have young people who
don't say a word. They're just like, 'Whatever . . . I
don't want to be here, I don't want to deal with this.'
When the talking piece goes around, young people
talk much more. The talking piece gives them both
the opportunity and a turn. It is very clearly defined:
'This is your space now.' Somehow this idea of the
talking piece, it's . . . I don't want to say profound, but
it gives the person holding it the ability to suddenly
say, 'Well, maybe I do have something to say.'"

SUSAN, ROCA STAFF

"I've noticed that for the first couple of Circles, a young
person might not talk, but by the third or fourth
Circle, they are really talking and expressing themselves, and I think that also translates to when they
are outside Circle. The Circle plays such a supportive
role. It's like, 'Okay, I'm valued, I'm respected . . . and if
people in the Circle can listen to what I have to say, so
can others, even if I'm outside of Circle.'"

VICTOR, ROCA STAFF

The Circle brings out the voices of young people, inviting them into existence. Each person gets an equal chance and opportunity to make his or her voice heard. Because the talking piece continually goes around the Circle, the invitation and opportunity to participate remain protected for each person. Individuals may decline to speak when the talking piece comes to them, but the opportunity to make their voices heard remains fundamentally theirs. The next time the talking piece comes around, the group sits ready to listen.

Over time, young people come to trust the safety that the Circle offers, and as they do, they find their voices. The moment comes when the Circle becomes a genuinely safe place to express deep or difficult emotions and experiences. At this point, the Circle becomes a process unlike any other: young people recognize this, and they begin to use the Circle for their own reasons. Voice and empowerment go hand in hand. Young people turn to Circles on their own and request Circles to address their own needs for healing, communication, or problem-solving with the people in their lives.

> "So, now it's working. They are finding ways for Circles to happen in their lives. I have a kid who wants to have a Circle with his teacher, because he feels like his teacher isn't any help to him. The kid was in a gang and jumped out recently. 'He [the teacher] looks at me as if I was a street kid. He asks every other student, "How are you doing today?" but he never asks me, "How am I doing today?" And I really want a Circle to talk about it.' He wants to explain to his teacher what it means to come to Roca and feel important and then go to school and feel like no one is listening."
>
> ANGIE, ROCA STAFF WORKER

When this young person asked Roca's staff to arrange a Circle with his teacher at school, he was turning to the Circle as a healthy way to have an important and difficult conversation with an adult. The young man felt that the teacher was treating him unfairly, ignoring him, and stereotyping him for his prior gang involvement. The Circle offered a respectful way for him to share those feelings with an adult in an environment where the young man believed he would be fully and fairly heard. It also offered a safe place for the teacher to acknowledge the young man's feelings without being attacked, accused, or blamed. The "we" of the Circle process—including the shared recognition that everyone is accountable for creating a positive future—shifts the process away from finger-pointing and opens an avenue for mutual accountability.

It is a tribute to Roca's learning journey that the young people now take the initiative to use the Circle in ways that serve their own needs: with each other; in their relationships with adults; for their own healing; and to celebrate their own lives, dreams, and futures. Young people are finding ways to make Circles do for them what they need them to do. Their initiatives demonstrate that those engaged in the Circle work have digested the Circle's deep lessons enough so that they can now hold the space for both young people and others in the community to come together on their own in a good way.

All Gifts Are Needed: The Circle as a Space of Belonging and Generosity

The dominant American culture assumes that our development as an individual puts us in conflict with our community or group. Presumably, we cannot be both an individual and connected to a group. In order to become an adult, then, the belief is that a person must separate from the group. This separation is assumed to be essential for the individual's growth, and adolescence is when this separation is supposed to occur. It is when young people are expected to reject adults in order to become who they really are.

Yet, according to many feminist and non-Western theorists, this notion is false. The individual and the group are not inevitably opposed. Being in relationship does not mean that we as individuals are swallowed up by a powerful group identity. To the contrary, our healthy development as individuals depends on our relationships with others. Indeed, our relationships with groups nourish us and call forth our individualities in all their power and uniqueness.

The experience of belonging is not, therefore, about suppressing individuality. It is about having one's individuality recognized by others. Roca cultivates a sense of belonging precisely to help young people thrive and grow. This is the same kind of cultivation that takes place within healthy families. In both environments, the group serves as an authentic mirror for reflecting back to individuals their special gifts and contributions.

In these situations, belonging is not about demanding uniformity or conformity to a single group identity. Quite the opposite: it is about acknowledging and understanding who we are as distinct and valued beings precisely by being in relationship with others. When others appreciate our talents, our thoughts, our sense of humor, and our passions, we experience being seen for who we are. Cultivating individuals depends on the group, and in turn, the diverse nature of individuals strengthens the group. In the natural world—of which we are, after all, a part—diversity is a source of stability, resilience, and vitality. So it is for human beings as well.

Circles bring out not only our differences but also what we have in common. In Circles, we become keenly aware of both simultaneously. When people from diverse backgrounds share their stories, they convey to others how distinct their experiences and histories have been. Those who listen can then empathize with the storytellers. Our capacity to do this—to witness and appreciate the meaning and emotion of another human experience, however different it may be from our own—is rooted in what we share as human beings. Being in Circle, therefore, helps us hold these two things in balance: what we have in common with how deeply we are also different. By participating in Circles, we build bridges and form communities. As we do, we also nurture and strengthen our unique experiences as individuals.

> "I was keeping a Circle for a group of Bosnian young men. A lot of them were heavily into Ecstasy—taking pills and other drugs too—so we did a Circle about substance abuse. There must have been about twenty of them. This is a group that did not listen to any-one: they were always rowdy, jumping up and down, making fun of each other, making fun of everybody. But for the first time, they were very quiet, and one person spoke at a time.
>
> "Right away, the stories went to their country, which is at war, and they started talking about their childhood. This is why they use drugs—to get away from the past. There was a lot of crying and sharing. I shared a lot too. What I learned was that we have a lot in common. They came from across the ocean, but they are dealing with things in almost the same way that I have dealt with my problems—by running away and using methods to run away from problems and not taking the opportunity to even talk about it. I learned that even though we grew up differently, we grew up with the same emotions."
>
> JAMES, ROCA STAFF

Like many Indigenous Peoples, the Ojibwe teach that all children are born with gifts and that it is the responsibility of adults to appreciate these gifts and to take part in developing them. Roca's

Roca youth

commitment to the value of generosity expresses this same idea: each young person has something of value to offer others. In the Circle space, the gift that each person is can be brought forth, appreciated, and expressed. Each person sits in a slightly different spot and views the issue through the lens of his or her own particular history and experiences. To truly understand an issue, we need all angles. What one person hears and "sees" in an issue differs from what someone else may hear or see. Each person's specific history affects what he or she notices and finds important.

From different stages of the life cycle, for example, people pay attention to different aspects of a story. The Circle as a whole is richer when older and younger people listen to each other's viewpoints. The wonder of it is that we each have our own ways of responding. Some individuals respond with humor, others with emotion; some speak at length, while others express themselves with only a few words or even a gesture. The Circle's wisdom lies in allowing all of this richness to come out and contribute to the fullest understanding of an issue. The Circle's beauty emerges as all of these qualities converge to form a whole that is greater than the mere sum of its parts.

> "In one Circle, this woman was talking about the tough time she was having with her daughter, who I think is twelve or thirteen. Her family had moved to this country and was having tough times. She felt she had failed as a mother. Her daughter was rebelling, and she felt that all the love and everything she had done for her daughter until this point had failed. Hearing this, I suddenly remembered the torture I put my mother through. I remembered hearing my mother say those same words: 'I'm a failure as a mother.' Something in my head just tipped. This poor woman! What can I say to her to get her through this time? Now that I'm older, my mother is my best friend. So I told a story about when I was in high school.
>
> "Now when I see this mother at Roca, she says, 'I remember what you said, and I tried some things that you suggested, and things are going better, and my daughter is coming around.' And when we sat in another Circle a couple of months ago, she brought a letter that her daughter had written to her apologizing for all the things she's been doing lately. It just comes down to the fact that we're all the same—you know what I mean?"
>
> A DEPARTMENT OF YOUTH SERVICES WORKER

When people share their stories in a Circle, they offer gifts of great value to others. In the stories, we hear parts of ourselves; we recognize things from our own past and hear our children or our parents through the experiences of others. We realize that we are not alone in having trouble, confusion, or pain. Equally, the lessons we may have learned from painful times or the mistakes we may have made can be a great help to others.

In this case, a young woman just beginning her adulthood offered her story as a gift to a mother and daughter in a place of conflict and separation. The perspective of the twenty-something young woman was a gift to both the woman and her daughter, because it helped them in the journey of their relationship. In turn, hearing their story reminded the young woman of the need to honor her own mother and the once tumultuous journey they had taken together.

The beauty of the Circle is that we all have these stories, because we are all human. The more we share our humanity with each other, the more we draw on the collective wisdom we possess as a community. Like Dorothy in *The Wizard of Oz*, the power to "go home" is with us all along. It is right here in ordinary people, but we seldom access it, largely because of the isolating ways we are set up to live. The Circle opens a space where the stories of our lives can once again mingle and guide us with the collective wisdom otherwise hidden among us.

CHAPTER FIVE

The Circle as a Space of Accountability

"The more you are physically sitting in Circle,
the more you get to be in Circle when you're not
in Circle."

VICTIM ADVOCATE, DISTRICT ATTORNEY'S OFFICE

Practicing mutual accountability is a critical element of Roca's success in working with young people. Yet what does practicing mutual accountability mean? How does it work? We hear the term "accountability" tossed around in our society, especially in regard to young people. In many cases, though, the term is used to justify policies that undermine the core values of Roca's mission and of those who use Circles as a way of life.

To understand the kind of accountability that Circles foster, we need to return once again to the core values guiding Roca's work: belonging, generosity, competence, and independence. Linked to the four sides of the Medicine Wheel and the four aspects of human beings, all four values affect the lives of young people, and all are necessary for young people to thrive. Belonging and generosity provide the foundation for young people's well-being, because they enable the youth to trust others and themselves. Young people must first believe, "I belong in this world" and "I have something to give."

Yet belonging and generosity alone are not enough. Young people need a whole range of competencies to exercise autonomy. The basic abilities to trust and be trustworthy provide the inner assurance that young people need to develop their competence in different areas. Specifically, they must acquire concrete knowledge, such as numeracy, literacy, basic life proficiencies, and other so-called hard skills. They must also develop social and interpersonal skills to communicate and to cooperate with others in a range of social settings. Certainly they must be able to establish healthy bonds of intimacy with a partner and their children. The so-called soft skills are as important to competence and independence as are the "hard skills" of reading, writing, and arithmetic. These skills of emotional intelligence develop the more we become aware of our own behavior and its impact on others.

Lastly, to grow into mature adults—emotionally, economically, and socially—young people need to be able to set personal goals, control their behavior, and plan for the future. Fundamentally, they must develop a vision of a positive future for themselves. As they do, they must also develop the capacity to plan actions that will make this vision a reality.

How do Circles help young people do all this? What does sitting in Circle have to do with showing up for a job as a cashier or being a student in a night computer class? Can sitting in Circle help a young person learn how to be a responsible parent, daughter, student, employee, or community member? It certainly can, namely, by generating an active, self-motivated commitment to holding oneself accountable. The values of the Circle and the kind of relationships that develop in Circles create a space where people naturally practice accountability—to themselves and each other. In other words, based on the values of belonging and generosity, Circles promote competence and independence by developing young people's ability to hold themselves accountable.

Accountability as Key to Competence and Independence

What is accountability, and why is it so central to the positive development of young people? In Western society, we have come

A Circle of youth at Roca

to associate accountability with punishment. When we hold so-and-so accountable for a wrong, we are often referring to some kind of sanction or penalty that is forcibly imposed. But genuine accountability is an active experience, not a passive one.[1] It is something we do, not something done to us.

Responsible adulthood requires that we become actively accountable. We fulfill our commitments and obligations; we admit wrongdoing; and we accept the consequences of our actions. In other words, becoming a mature adult means routinely taking responsibility for what we do. We truthfully acknowledge the impact of our behavior on others, take positive steps to repair any harm we cause, and make efforts to prevent harms from recurring.

These core habits of accountability are equally important to developing competence and independence. We need these habits to hold a job, support a family, be a citizen, and care for ourselves. Helping young people learn habits of accountability is one of the missing pieces of modern social development that Circles help to restore. As with the path to maturity, learning to be accountable does not happen all at once with an abrupt insight or sudden revelation. It is a long, steady learning process. No matter how many stumbles young people may make along the way, they gradually make changes in their behavior, until they discover that they can be accountable.

Also like the maturation process, we learn accountability in relationship with others. Young people need to interact with supportive, caring adults who can help them develop the habits that accountability requires. Adults encourage young people, for example, to reflect honestly on their own behavior and to become aware of the impact of what they do on others. When harms occur, adults help youth seek opportunities for making apologies, find ways to put things right and make amends, and allow themselves to start anew with fresh insights.

Adults in our society fail young people when they deny them the opportunity to learn and grow from mistakes. Our society has little tolerance for the mistakes that at-risk youth often make. The concept of zero-tolerance rejects the idea of mistakes as opportunities for growth. Instead, this philosophy relies on fear to motivate good behavior. Yet who thrives in a climate of fear? How can we ever grow if we cannot use mistakes as chances to learn?

Equally damaging for youth is the choice adults sometimes make to refrain from sharing their own learning experiences. Everyone makes mistakes in life, and most life journeys are neither straight nor easy. When adults present themselves as finished products of perfect behavior, many young people—who may already feel isolated and alone—feel overwhelmed by their own mistakes. They quickly conclude that they are hopelessly inadequate or so far from who they should be that it is futile for them to try to change. Adults who have "been there, done that" and are willing to share their stories in Circle without lecturing or imposing judgments offer an enormously refreshing and motivating source of support and guidance for young people.

Sitting in Circle begins a journey of accountability to one's self and the community, and it greatly affects people's lives and relationships. Since the Circle is about practicing a different way to be in the world based on a commitment to values, Circle participants naturally model how they hold themselves accountable for their actions many times and in many situations. Young people notice this. They learn how to act in a good way by continually trying to live up to the Circle values, so that they can be in greater harmony with others and themselves.

The process of becoming accountable is not, therefore, an act of critical judgment or an excuse to shame, punish, or belittle others. Nor is it about holding up an unrealistic state of perfection as a way to condemn young people for not measuring up. In Circles, accountability is seen as part of everyday life. Adults support youth by sharing their own daily struggles around holding themselves accountable. Sitting in Circle has taught those at Roca a great deal about the many kinds of accountability that young people and communities need to thrive. Moreover, surrounded by injustices, the young people are learning that accountability to one's self, to others, and to the wider community is what true justice requires.

> "So there are all these life lessons in Circles around what it means to be in the world and what it means to walk in the world in a good way. Using Circle to prepare for employment is so appropriate, because they are learning how to be in the world, and Circles are the way to really capture that. What does it mean to be in a good way? To not be angry, pissed off, and bitter, because that is how they act a lot of the time. Really, it's giving them an opportunity to experience what it means to be in a good way, which will transfer over to everything that they ever do in employment. It's really an opportunity for young people to identify these overarching guidelines of living."
>
> SUSAN, ROCA STAFF

Deciding How to Live

Creating guidelines is an integral part of the Circle process. In fact, it distinguishes the profoundly different nature of this space from other social spaces. This feature of Circles carries special significance for young people. Again, Circle guidelines are a set of values that participants identify, discuss, and agree upon as part of the Circle process. Unlike rules that are en-

Roca youth

forced by those with authority, the guidelines express how the people sitting in the Circle collectively wish to be with each other. In every Circle, the group must come to an agreement about which values will govern their treatment of each other during the Circle. For many young people, the chance to talk about how they are expected to behave is a powerful shift away from the familiar structure of authority.

> "In schools, adults are never flexible, and young people
> are never given the space to decide for themselves what
> the rules are or to have the idea that they can change
> those rules. Wow! To say, 'I don't agree to this' and
> to know that the rules would change for me or that I
> can challenge them? They don't experience this in the
> schools or their homes or anywhere else in their lives."
>
> LIZ, ROCA STAFF

Young people are seldom given an opportunity to discuss—much less come to an agreement about—the rules that they are asked to obey. But in Circles, coming to an agreement about a Circle's guidelines is vital to the process. In fact, the process can be quite lengthy and complex because it requires consensus, which in turn requires genuine discussion about each desired behavior. As the talking piece goes around and around the Circle, participants grapple with such questions as:

- Is a particular value worth desiring and acting on? Why or why not?
- What standards or rules should we live by? Why do we want to live this way?
- What is so important about respect? honesty? compassion?
- If a guideline asks that people respect confidentiality, does this include all kinds of discussions? What about adults who may be mandated reporters?
- Do the guidelines apply to everyone?
- Do they apply in all situations? If there is a guideline that asks people to be honest, for example, does it mean we must be honest even when it is hurtful?
- Showing respect may be an important guideline for the Circle, but how do we really practice respect?

Agreeing on guidelines gives young people an experience of genuine democratic participation that they find almost nowhere else in their lives. It can be overwhelmingly discouraging for young people to face a world full of rules that are established by adults with little flexibility, explanation, or input from them. Nobody enjoys being simply "told" what the rules are and constantly reminded of the bad things that will happen to us if we fail to obey them even in the slightest. Circles offer young people a radically different experience.

> "In the Circle, it's not like they have no choice and are told, 'Here, this is what you have to do. These are the guidelines, and that's that; you have to abide by them

now.' No! In Circle, they have a say as to the meaning
of it, and at the same time, they can change them and
challenge them. They have the choice."

LIZ, ROCA STAFF

It is not unusual for a Circle with young people to spend hours or
even days discussing guidelines. In a series of Circles for thirty
young people at Youth Star (an AmeriCorps program at Roca), the
group spent two whole days—four to six hours each day—*just
talking about guidelines*. In talking Circles with gang members, the
guidelines discussion often focuses on the meaning of a few core
values: What does respect mean to you? What does love mean
to you? What does confidentiality mean? Agreeing on a Circle's
guidelines involves a deep discussion about the meaning of these
values and the concrete implications of acting on them. This may
be the first time that young people really talk with adults—or
even each other—about how to show love or what it means to be
respected.

Whereas the Indigenous idea of guidelines stems from a
spiritual understanding of law that reflects the cosmic order, the
Western concept of rule-based law is human centered. It is a col-
lection of man-made strictures that carry out the authority of the
state. They help us know what is expected in terms of good behavior and which behaviors are not acceptable. Most of us tend to
think of rules as prohibitions on wrong conduct, such as stealing
or swearing. We even go a step further and assume that rules have
no power if they are not enforced—that is, if failure to follow
them is not punished by those in authority. In modern societies,
those who are in positions of authority, such as the police or the
courts, have the job of punishing those who fail to comply.

Guidelines work differently. Forged through an inclusive and
thorough dialogue, a Circle's guidelines represent wise counsel
about how to live well with one's self and others. They are less
about what we shouldn't do and more about what we should do

in all our relationships, including with ourselves. Instead of representing specific rules to be enforced, guidelines express important values to be practiced.

In modern society, articulating values and their meaning for our lives is a conversation ordinary people rarely have with one another. These discussions have been taken over by professionals. For those familiar with restorative justice theory, one core insight is that the state has, in fact, "stolen" our conflicts. Individuals and communities no longer deal with breakdowns in our relationships, families, and communities. Instead, we are told to rely on lawyers and other justice professionals. They are supposed to resolve our harms and differences for us and to deliver justice.

With the loss of our power to decide how to handle our conflicts, we have also lost our role in deciding which values we want to live by as a people, especially when conflicts and harms arise. In contemporary society, "values talk" is left to speech-makers, politicians, clergy, talk-show hosts, and publicists. These discussions are not dialogues but monologues: the few do the talking, while the many are silent.

But even in personal life, how often do adults have candid, honest discussions with young people about the values underlying one behavior or another? How often do adults share with young people their own struggles with practicing good values every day? The words that name our values often become empty phrases disconnected from daily life.

When we stop talking about fundamental questions of meaning and values, we are no longer able to give young people the practical advice they need about how to live in a good way. Our silence in regard to values leaves them vulnerable to the onslaught of messages from the entertainment industry, which glamorizes values of violence, power, greed, dishonesty, and manipulation. Young people live in an absurdly dualistic, disjointed world as far as values are concerned. Fictional adults incessantly hype values that are cynical, highly dysfunctional for most human relationships, and downright nihilistic, while real-life adults often remain strangely silent when it comes to talking about the most important issues in life. Many young people grow up with a sense of despair, confusion, and distrust in the world of adults.

Practicing the Guidelines: A Lesson in Accountability

> "There's already accountability in coming to Circle—
> of how you're gonna be in the Circle. There are all
> these values that you always have to hold and try to
> live by, so there's already accountability there."
>
> JAMES, ROCA STAFF

The Circle's opening lesson in accountability is that each participant is personally accountable for upholding the guidelines of the Circle. For many young people, being held accountable means being subjected to threats and punishments. It comes as quite a revelation, then, when they realize that it is up to each participant to choose to follow the guidelines. The character and quality of the Circle space depends entirely on the degree to which participants do this.

For example, the Circle is a place of respect insofar as those involved are respectful; it is confidential if participants preserve confidentiality; everyone will be heard if others listen. The guidelines work to the degree that the people in the Circle decide to be that way with each other. As simple as this lesson is, it teaches many Circle participants, young and old, a great deal about accountability. If living in accordance with key values is something we wish for, then it is also something that we must be responsible for.

Saroeum recalls one of the first Circles ever held at Roca— one that had a powerful impact on him and everyone else as well. There had been a fight between two young women that began when one girl assaulted another. The conflict escalated, generating enormous tensions within a group of young people. They

Roca youth

decided to sit everyone in the program—about thirty young people—in a Circle. Saroeum's only thought at the time was to "trust
the process." They did an opening, and then they began to talk
about guidelines.

> "We went about six rounds on guidelines. . . . There
> were probably close to a hundred-plus guidelines—
> respect, love, no swearing, no yelling, no racial com-
> ments, everything—and it kept going and going. In
> my head, I am saying, 'How the hell are we gonna live
> these guidelines?' One young woman was so opposed
> to Circle. She said, 'Well, how in the world are we
> gonna respect these guidelines because there are so
> many of them, and I don't think the Circle thing is
> working.' So she keeps pushing that this Circle thing
> is not working. . . . By this time, I'm almost ready
> to give up, thinking, 'Can't we just go back to deal-
> ing with things in the usual way, you know . . . just

talking trash to people and threatening them to resolve issues.'

"So somewhere, somehow, I was just humble in that state, and I got up and said, 'Well, who in this room feels uncomfortable about these guidelines? Can we talk about that?' Then I just gave the feather away, and it just went, and I think that things started to shift from that moment. Instead of people saying general stuff, they started saying, 'Well, people are fighting already, and I don't know if we can respect each other. . . .' and there was talk like, 'Well, I don't know about this "no swearing," 'cause if people are swearing at me, I might need to swear back.' It took the whole day—I mean four, five, six hours—just to talk about guidelines."

SAROEUM, ROCA STAFF

At that moment, the young people began to take the guidelines seriously: What would it mean to act respectfully toward one another? How can you do that if you are angry or if others are not respectful toward you? Rather than regarding values as just words on a page, the young people in the Circle began to discuss what it would really mean to practice these values with one another. They realized that no one was able to enforce these values except themselves: it was up to them.

The lesson in accountability inherent in the guidelines created a powerful opening for the two girls who had had the fight. They discovered that it was in their power to be accountable to themselves and each other—a power they had never before realized that they had. The shift toward being responsible for practicing the values opened a space for each girl to share her feelings honestly and without anger. It created an opening for understanding and, ultimately, reconciliation.

"So we created that gentleness and that place to a point where finally it was comfortable to talk with each other. And the young woman who first punched the other, she's the one who first apologized to the other girl and to everybody. When the talking piece got to her, she said, 'Look, I'm really sorry about what I did, that I physically punched you in the face, 'cause I was having a hard time with my mom. She is so sick to a point where she might not make it, and my baby was really sick at the same time, and I didn't get enough sleep, and you kept harassing me, and I told you about ten times to stop what you were doing.'

"So she was very courageous in coming forward, and then everybody started apologizing to one another as we went around. Then it gets to the woman who got decked in the face, and she says, 'Look, Jesus, I'm really sorry. I didn't know your mom was really sick or that your baby was sick, 'cause we always play around like that, and I thought it was okay.' Well, my eyes were tearing up, and it just keeps going around and someone got up and gave someone a hug and someone else got up, and then it was a big group hug and a big group forgiveness."

SAROEUM, ROCA STAFF

Agreeing on guidelines and then holding ourselves to them have proven to be a profoundly important experience for the young people at Roca. The Circle's core lesson is that the guidelines actually reflect the values that the participants in a particular Circle choose to share in determining how they want to be together. Participants can talk about values and come to an understanding about what they mean, but only when people commit to living those values do the guidelines have real power. The lesson of the guidelines, then, is that what we want and hope for ourselves and our community will become real only when we—each person in the Circle—choose to live our values ourselves and with each other.

Circles as a Space for Change

> *Jose dropped out of high school and was heavily involved with gangs and drugs when he began to show up at Roca. Although he had worked in various manual jobs, he regularly lost these jobs when he failed to show up, fought on the job, or came to work high. At Roca, a streetworker asked Jose about his vision for his future. "What vision?" He never thought about the future. There was nothing in the world that he cared about—nothing at all.*
>
> *Yet he continued to show up at Roca, participating in Circles, working out in the weight room, and forming close relationships with streetworkers. Slowly, he began to articulate a desire to leave the gang life. His girlfriend became pregnant, and through the conversations with Roca staff and in Circle, he began to imagine a different kind of life for himself and to make small steps toward change. Roca helped get him a job as a busboy at a local restaurant and periodically checked in with his supervisor in the kitchen. Before long, the supervisor informed Roca that Jose was coming late and had begun talking loudly about gangs at work. As an ex-gang member himself, the supervisor knew where that kind of talk would lead. The supervisor warned Roca that it would not be long before Jose would be fired.*
>
> *In one-on-one conversations and in Circles, Roca staff shared this feedback with Jose: Is this behavior going to help him get what he really wants for his future? Is this who he really wants to be? Jose began to act more responsibly. He held that restaurant job for eight months, and then decided he*

wanted a better job. He found an opening in construction and asked advice on how to interview and inquire about hours, pay, and other aspects of the job. He went out to lunch with the supervisor and successfully negotiated the job.

Jose was working at this job for several months when he broke up with his girlfriend. Suddenly a lot of old behaviors returned: drug use, not showing up, and spending more time on the street with the gang. In danger of losing his job again, people in Circles and at Roca reminded Jose of his vision for himself and how happy he was when he was working and living with his girlfriend. They encouraged him to make up with her and go back to the life he was living with her. Jose followed their advice and returned both to work and to his girlfriend. While not officially out of the gang, Jose spends little time with them. He works full time and lives with his girlfriend, regularly attending Circles with other young men and women at Roca.

Circles promote accountability in three interrelated ways:

1. They provide a space where modeling takes place. Young people learn vital lessons from hearing stories from peers and adults about how they learned to live responsibly and what this really means.
2. Through this exposure, Circles offer a space where young people can begin to develop a vision of themselves in the future.
3. Circles support young people as they do the concrete work of turning their visions into realities. Support from the Circle is reliably there as they take the countless small steps necessary to achieve major life changes.

These three practices—gaining wisdom by witnessing the journey of others; creating a vision of oneself in the company of others;

and receiving constant support in making the incremental steps toward realizing one's own vision—are why Circles have such positive effects in the lives of young people. They offer practical assistance in the awesome daily struggle to grow and develop in the world.

It Begins with Vision

> "Once they can say, 'I belong in the world,' then the next step is, 'Well, if I belong in the world, I'm gonna need some sort of roadmap to get me where I want to go. I'm gonna need a vision.'"
>
> SUSAN, ROCA STAFF

In many Indigenous societies, young people on the brink of adulthood retreat to a place in the natural world to reflect on who they are and what their particular purpose in this life might be. During their vision quest, they are supported by their families and communities, who pray for them. The vision they receive helps guide them as they embark on their adult lives, providing clarity when they need to make choices. The vision is shared with others, who then support them in understanding their vision and living by it. The vision becomes part of their identity and serves as a reminder of their core self when life gets muddled or hard.

Young people everywhere are desperate for a vision of themselves as competent, deserving, purposeful, and valued members of a group. Before they can pursue a journey of transformation, they must develop a vision of who they really want to be—a vision that is rooted in a belief about who they really are.

Developing such a vision and then living it is not something we do in isolation. It is an interactive, collaborative process. We all gain a sense of who we are through our relationships, which mirror to us various images and aspects of who we are. From a young age through late adolescence and early adulthood, young

Roca youth

people who are fortunate enough to have caring, adult support are often asked to imagine their future. "Who do you want to be when you grow up?" is a visioning question that they are encouraged to ponder again and again in dialogues with caring adults as they mature.

Young people growing up without the supportive presence of adults are unfamiliar with this kind of thinking. Most of the messages they receive communicate a negative view of who they are and what they bring to the world. If their dreams exist at all, they are shaped by unrealistic images from the media, disconnected from real choices and opportunities. A sense of cynicism about their life's possibilities pervades their thinking, making them disbelieve that they could ever attain a future for themselves different from what they see around them.

Preparing young people to be self-sufficient begins with interrupting these habits of thought. It means providing opportunities for young people to hope for a different future and then helping them walk toward making their dreams into realities. Transformational relationships and Circles do precisely that. Through the relationships that form in these contexts, young people begin to re-vision their lives and shift how they see themselves and their futures.

What will carry young people forward not just six months from now but also six years from now as they face new obstacles and struggles? Indigenous societies are right: to continually move in positive directions, young people need a vision. It is the vision of themselves and their future that keeps them on track. As they mature, they gain the self-worth and skills not only to imagine a different future but also to make it happen.

> "At the time we started the visioning in Circles, my goal was to get my daughter into daycare. You write down the steps to get you toward that, and when you get it done, you put a little gold star next to it. You do this just so you get used to making goals and following through with them. So I got my daughter into daycare. I had it in the book and made the steps. If you keep a promise to yourself, sometimes people don't follow through with it, but this helps you stay with it, so you can work toward something bigger.
>
> "In later Circles, we made posters about our goals in five years—where we want to live and what house we want to have. It's good, 'cause it gets you thinking a lot about the goals you want for yourself. I am going to start as a medical assistant, and while doing that, I'll work on being a nurse. I had an idea before that I wanted to do this, but I didn't really have a sense of how I was going to get there. I took away a good feeling that I can do this: If I say I can, I can."
>
> A NINETEEN-YEAR-OLD SINGLE MOTHER AT ROCA

Using Circles to Support Incremental Shifts in Habits

> "Let's say a young person expresses that he wants to
> go back to school. We come to agreement in that Circle
> that he's gonna do certain things so he can go back to
> school, and if he doesn't live up to what he's supposed
> to do, then we need to talk about that in the Circle. The
> Circle does hold each individual accountable. That's the
> beauty of it, because everyone has their own respon-
> sibility, but that responsibility is shared by everybody
> else. I don't think you can get that anywhere else."
>
> JAMES, ROCA STAFF

John Braithwaite's vision of "youth development Circles,"[2] which
I mentioned earlier, offers a social innovation that may well prove
essential today, because it addresses a structural gap in supportive relationships for many young people. Parents carry the entire
burden of nurturing and supporting their children. Even under
the best of circumstances, they can easily become overextended
as the sole support structure for youth.

When parents are unable to meet their children's needs, the
only adults left to care for them are those who are "paid to care."
These people are typically staff employed within formal bureaucratic institutions, such as schools, social services, and juvenile
justice agencies. Yet, the way these institutions are structured
makes them far too impersonal. They cannot provide the moral
support and individual guidance that youth desperately need to
develop in positive directions.

> "There are generations of young people who don't
> have the skills necessary—primarily the soft skills:
> working with other people, appropriate attire, man-
> aging time, managing stress, the balance between
> home and work. I mean, all of these things are very

foreign. So how do you hold lines for somebody who doesn't know where the lines are? Well, first, we teach them where the lines are, and I am very clear: these are the things that are appropriate in work, and these are the things that are not appropriate in work. We need to teach these things."

SUSAN, ROCA STAFF

Circles help young people grow not only by helping them understand what they want to change about their lives but also by making their intentions known to a group of people who are willing to support them in making those changes happen. Circles help young people develop concrete plans and stick to them so that they can reach their goals, even long-term ones. In addition to cultivating one-on-one relationships, Circles call on the support of a wider community. They build meaningful connections among young people as well as with a network of adults, all of whom stand ready to offer concrete assistance.

Circles promote two particularly important activities that young people need to engage with the world successfully: reflection and practice. *Reflection* has been described as the consummate soft skill. Being aware of ourselves, our environment, and how others perceive us are essential skills for navigating our way around society and "fitting in" in a variety of settings. By expanding our self-awareness, reflective skills open us to new possibilities, which in turn expand our options for making choices. Quite simply, Circles provide a space where—in the company of others—young people can reflect on who they are and who they would like to become.

"I think Circles help people see a lot about themselves. Some young people might not speak loudly in words but their actions speak much louder. They drop out and get heavily into gangs. Circles help them

start to see what they need to do for themselves.
And when people start sharing, it sort of clicks in
their head: 'Oh wow! What am I doing? This is so
ridiculous. What do I need to do? What do I need
to do to be accountable?' We just ask the questions.
We are not telling them what to do. We are sharing
what we think we need to do to be accountable and
responsible."

LIZ, ROCA STAFF

Circles are also a place to *practice* the soft skills required for competence and independence. The Circle itself is a highly behavioral setting. Being in Circle means following the guidelines, which are all about how each person thinks and behaves. Circles reinforce lessons of self-control, appropriate conduct, and meeting one's commitments. The guidelines and rituals of the Circle require relatively high levels of self-discipline, patience, and conformity unique to this setting.

"Circle is a space that reinforces a lot of the things
that we're trying to do. Guidelines are about how to
act appropriately in certain spaces. The Circle reinforces that idea. I'm sitting here and telling them:
this is appropriate in work; that is inappropriate in
work. When you sit in Circle, the Circle creates guidelines. The guidelines create what is appropriate in the
Circle, so it gives them a chance to practice appropriate behavior."

SUSAN, ROCA STAFF

Modeling Accountability

A sixteen-year-old girl and her mother came together in a series of Circles to address drug abuse and her failure to attend school. Referred by DSS and the courts to Roca, the daughter was following in the footsteps of her mother, who modeled behavior she had witnessed through much of her childhood and adolescence. In the Circle, the mother, now sober, apologized to her daughter and painfully took responsibility for the mistakes she had made for herself and her daughter.

This was an emotional turning point for the daughter, who proceeded to use the support of the Circle to make the behavioral changes she wanted to make in her own life. With the support of the Circle, she stopped using drugs, got a part-time job, and earned her GED. Monthly Circles provided continual support for both mother and daughter, as both continued to make concrete, positive changes in their lives and their relationship.

Very often, adults use a double standard: one for the behaviors they expect of young people and another for the behaviors they expect of themselves. When adults give lip service to a set of values but fail to model them in their own behavior, young people notice at once. They are very sensitive to hypocrisy in adult conduct. When they perceive a gap between preaching and practice, they find it hard to trust adults, much less learn from them. Their sensitivity to such discrepancies makes sense, because adult hypocrisy forces youth to make a choice: "Do I do what they say, or do I do what they do?"

Young people crave real guidance—not platitudes or lecturing. The importance of sharing our stories as adults bears repeating: when adults pretend that we are without flaws or struggles, we withhold from young people the very stories that could be of greatest value to them. Circles allow young people to witness our honest struggles to do the right thing, meet our obligations, change our own negative habits, and live up to our own and others' expectations.

For youth who have been neglected by adults, this kind of adult sharing demonstrates what the Circle is all about, and youth find it both instructive and healing. It teaches that all human beings make mistakes and that, with courage and determination, it is possible to begin again and make things right.

Circles Are about a Different Kind of Justice

> "To be in a good way with yourself is really to practice what you say in the Circle."
>
> VICHEY, ROCA STAFF

Vichey Phoung was born in a Thai refugee camp and was brought to this country as a baby. Life was not easy for the family when they arrived in Boston with five sons in 1984. The trauma of war, hunger, and loss left their mark on the adults and children. Despite having survived the horrors of war, they faced the emotional fallout of post-traumatic stress and were unable to cope with the many obstacles of American society. According to Vichey's older brother, Saroeum Phoung, "My parents and some older folks would not talk about what happened in Cambodia. They just keep it to themselves. That's why they get crazy. Our family didn't talk about it. I don't talk to anybody. My father doesn't talk to anybody. Everybody just shuts their mouth. Before, we stuck together as a family. And when we came to this country . . . like, damn, we're in the land of making a dream come true, and then we split."

Vichey's parents divorced after his father lost the family's savings through chronic bouts of drinking and gambling. Like his father, Vichey began to drink heavily to cope with emotional pain and frustration, and like his older brothers, he found community on the street with a gang of other young Cambodian men. At the age of twenty-one, Vichey pled guilty

to assault with a dangerous weapon. Originally charged with
attempted murder, Vichey gained a plea agreement when the
victim and witnesses refused to testify against him.

In the eyes of the dominant society, Vichey was held accountable
for his actions the moment he was convicted of the crime and required by the court to serve time behind bars. The prevailing concept of justice in American society focuses on imposing punishments following "due process." It includes little or no expectation
that an offender such as Vichey might choose to make amends
toward those he hurt. Nor does it include any role for the victims,
family members, neighbors, or anyone else directly involved in
the complex incident that led to conviction.

Instead, our system of justice isolates a particular event—the
crime—from the history, context, and relationships of the participants. The system hears only the legal charges and the "facts"
that support those charges primarily from its own representa-
tives, namely, the lawyers. It then passes judgment on the individual based on this narrowly selected and packaged set of information. A sentence is imposed, and "justice is served."

Yet this dominant Euro-American model is by no means the
only understanding of justice. Restorative justice presents a much
wider concept. It expects offenders to take active responsibility
for their actions; it involves victims in the process; and it seeks to
address the harm to all concerned and to repair the damage. This
wider frame for "doing justice" makes sense if we want to understand what went wrong, so that we can build a better foundation
for the future.

This broader approach to justice can be found in most pre-
modern and non-Western traditions. Restorative in both practice
and goals, the peacemaking Circle process is often used to bring
victims, offenders, their families, and the wider community together. Through the Circle process, participants seek to understand what happened and why. They then explore what actions

are needed to resolve the harm and to create the conditions for different behaviors in the future.

By the time Vichey was convicted in court, he had already embarked on a change process in his own life through his growing involvement in Roca and in peacemaking Circles. A quiet young man, he was often silent in the Circles, but he listened. He wasn't quite sure what he thought of the Circles, especially some of the strange rituals that participants often chose to use, like burning sage, but there was something about them that he liked, so he was willing to show up.

> "At first, it is weird—sitting in Circle, getting up,
> holding hands, especially with guys. It's very hard
> to hold hands and not giggle or say aloud, 'This is
> weird.' It's very hard at first, but after we go through
> it for a while, we feel, 'Okay, this is cool, people are
> listening.'"
>
> VICHEY, ROCA STAFF

When Roca asked Vichey if he would be willing to use the Circle to help take responsibility for what he had done, he cautiously agreed. In the months leading up to his sentencing hearing, Vichey participated in a series of Circles to address the harm he had caused to others and to himself. Thus, in a process separate from the formal justice system, Vichey agreed to be accountable to himself and his community through the Circle.

> "The Circle didn't lessen my time or help my case.
> I was meeting with the Circle just on my own, and
> those are the Circles I really didn't want to be in,
> 'cause they were so hard. You yourself acknowledge
> the harm of what you've done and the need to talk
> about it, who I've harmed, and what ripple effect it
> had. To be able to be in conversation about that stuff,

then to understand and be aware of it: only then do you hold yourself accountable."

VICHEY, ROCA STAFF

The Circle included members of Vichey's family who shared the same painful family history and had themselves struggled to overcome negative ways of dealing with their pain. Also in the Circle were Roca staff, Vichey's peers, and members of the community who were willing to show up and support Vichey. These community members included a local judge, a corrections professional, and a teacher, all of whom volunteered their time to support Vichey on his journey.

> "I mean, my mom worked so hard just to get me things and to target the American dream for me. Little did she know that I didn't really need all that. All I needed was some love and caring, and she didn't know that. All she did was try to put food on the table and clothe me and everything else, and she worked so hard that she was hardly ever there for me. I grew up with a single mom, so she was hardly ever there for me. I just found love and caring—not that she didn't love me—but I found that through the street life.
>
> "I wouldn't say I'm proud of that, but it's just at that moment in time when I was going through this that the streets sort of showed me the love and care that I was craving. And I was young as well and didn't understand much. So it was just that for me. I think it's pretty hard if you're raised in a different culture. Your mom grew up in a different world, and you grew up here. And when the communication is not there between your mom and you, it makes it very hard as well. And a lot of kids like me turn to the streets and

to our peers, because they knew my language and could speak my language. And they were doing the same thing and similar things, so it's very easy to get lost in the streets."

VICHEY, ROCA STAFF

Vichey's willingness to open himself and his story to others was a profound learning experience. It proved transformative not only for him but also for all who witnessed his growth toward holding himself accountable for his actions.

"It's a little bit difficult, because you don't normally share personal stuff. And sometimes I do break down and cry, and that's a new thing for me. At first, I didn't feel very comfortable explaining myself, but then as the healing Circle goes on, everyone is sharing, and everyone knows a little bit of each other."

VICHEY, ROCA STAFF

Vichey courageously confronted the pain he had caused others as well as his own suffering. The capacity of Circle participants both to sit with the truth of harm and simultaneously to support people with compassion and respect as they search for ways to make amends is powerful. It also offers great hope for communities who are suffering from many layers of injustice and harm, because it opens a path toward justice that is transformative and healing.

"Sitting in Circle with my brother [Vichey] was the big mind blower for me. I grew up with him and helped raise him in some ways. I think of him as the most shut down and reactive individual. His involvement in the gang was pretty intense, so I was not surprised at what he did, because I'm sure he watched

me a lot in my early years. We talked a lot during my
years on the street. He wanted to be like me. He was
proud of me for being a gang member and for being
the most vicious son of a bitch in town.

"So for him to be willing to work with the Circle—
to take whatever risk is necessary, to take that journey where he was so highly accountable and responsible that he was willing to go to jail for the harm
he caused, to hold himself accountable in a public
arena—I am so humbled by him. I think he is more
gifted than his older brother."

SAROEUM, VICHEY'S OLDER BROTHER AND ROCA STAFF

In court, Vichey was sentenced for his crime. In the Circle, Vichey
took responsibility for what he did within his own community. By
choosing to go to Circle, Vichey chose the hard path of confront-
ing the consequences of his behavior for the people in his life and
for his community. The full impact of his actions was revealed to
him. He came to understand what he was responsible for and why
he was being held accountable.

Accountability in the context of caring is essential in the journey toward justice, because it supports growth and transformation. What does "accountability in the context of caring" mean?
It means that others acknowledge their responsibility to offer
support and encouragement to those who face the challenges of
personal growth. It means that people are seen in their fullness.
It means that those who have done harm to others are identified
with more than their worst behaviors; all their actions—good and
bad—are acknowledged. The Circle weaves mutual caring with
mutual accountability, so that people are held in a good way. This
gives them the inner strength to step forward and take responsibility for a healing journey.

The court, by comparison, is a place where "offending" indi-

viduals come before the judgment of the state. They have no opportunity to express themselves; neither do they have the compassion, caring, or support of those who know their struggle and
pain. In New Zealand, the restorative practice of family group
conferencing has replaced courtroom encounters for juveniles,
because the Maori believe that such rituals of public condemna-
tion and isolation are both degrading and inhumane.

When Vichey stood before the judge at the sentencing hearing, the traditional courtroom discourse was deeply disparaging
of Vichey as a human being. For those who know and love Vichey,
this demonizing of him was painful to hear.

> "At the sentencing hearing, because we love him dearly
> and respect his growth so much, I got angry at the
> judge. We tried to tell the judge that Vichey had
> helped young men on Shirley Avenue stop fighting.
> The judge said, 'Well, he's a criminal, he shouldn't be
> on the street. He should be going to jail. I don't know
> why he is working at Roca. How can someone so
> negative work with youth?'
>
> "I was thinking, you don't know this young man! To
> hear that from the judge! I had a burning desire to go
> up there and grab him by the neck and say, 'You don't
> know this young man well enough to talk so negatively
> about him. You don't know what he has done in his
> life!' But at the time, Vichey said, 'It's okay. I'm gonna
> go to jail, and it'll be fine.' He accepted that.
>
> "That was most humbling, because he had talked
> in Circle about wanting to go to jail for his own ac-
> tions. In the Circle, he said, 'I wouldn't feel good if I
> was not going to jail.' So for him to do that with such
> courage, he's more human than ever."
>
> SAROEUM, VICHEY'S BROTHER AND ROCA STAFF

Most offenders never acknowledge or fully comprehend the impact of their actions on others. Nor are they offered the kind of support that would give them the courage and self-respect to stand up and hold themselves accountable to a community that passionately believes in them and wants them to succeed. For most people in our nation's jails and prisons, punishment is a passive experience imposed on them by the all-powerful criminal justice system. Most feel only anger and resentment toward the system for punishing them; few ever acknowledge responsibility for what they have done. And very few ever have the opportunity or the means to be genuinely accountable and to begin to change.

Vichey had the loving support of Roca and his community, and the Circle opened a path toward healing and accountability that truly changed this young man's life. For him, his time in jail was an act of genuine contrition that became part of a life-changing transformation.

> "I think the most powerful Circle I was in was when Vichey said, 'You know, I went to jail for what I had done, and I did some pretty serious stuff. And when I got to jail, I was the only person there who knew why I was there. I went to court, I didn't talk, the lawyers talked. The judge sentenced me, and I went to jail. And everybody in jail was either "innocent" or "wrong place, wrong time." Nobody really owned what they did. But I know what I did. I knew why I was there.'"
>
> GREGG, TEACHER AND COMMUNITY PARTNER

> "I think the Circle helped me become who I am today."
>
> VICHEY, ROCA STAFF

CHAPTER SIX

The Circle as a Space for Healing

"If kids have been hurt for a long time, you've got to stay the course to create a space for them to heal over a long time. It's not coming overnight. It's not a program you can put them through, fix 'em and spit 'em out, like, 'Okay, put 'em through the wash, all set, put 'em in the dryer, okay, we're getting this done. . . . Next!' It doesn't get 'done to' or 'fixed,' really."

MOLLY, ROCA'S EXECUTIVE DIRECTOR

"Healing, I think, is the hardest thing, but when the healing begins, it's the most important thing."

JAMES, ROCA STAFF

The need for healing is great within poor, minority, and immigrant communities. At Roca, young people and their families are deeply affected by systemic and generational cycles of violence and harm:

- They live in communities damaged by the wounds of war, violence, displacement, poverty, and pervasive institutional racism.
- They are raised in homes with painful histories of abuse, neglect, separation, poverty, drug and alcohol addiction, and emotional dysfunction.

Roca youth

- Many have fled war-torn countries or are children of survivors.
- They have experienced repeated failures and punitive discipline at school and are drug, gang, and street involved.
- Many have been locked up more than once in juvenile and adult correctional facilities.

Trauma of all kinds permeates the lives of young people at Roca. From a young age, they have borne the burden of violence in their lives and have learned to hide their pain or numb it with drugs or sex. Not surprisingly, in a self-defeating search for power and control, they often resort to violence themselves.

> "When we first started Circles, a lot of kids were getting distracted in the Circle. They didn't understand

the concept of Circles. They just didn't want to sit down, they didn't want to listen, they didn't want to go through these guidelines. So I said, 'Why don't we take them on a camping trip to a place where they don't know anyone and can't run away and have Circles there?' So we did.

"We started out having a lot of fun, played a lot of games. But in the nighttime, negative stuff started happening. Kids started wearing their bandanas, different gang colors, one person started getting mad at someone else and nearly had a fight. So I said, 'Well, we have to do a Circle now. Let's do it now.'

"It was so intense. There were about thirty-two kids in a huge Circle. We had a talking piece, sage. It was a four-hour Circle, and it was the first time kids actually sat down and for four hours talked about gangs, rape, school, teachers not understanding them, parents leaving them, foster homes, everything. There were kids who said that they were assaulted, raped; people who were afraid of killing other people and who had attempted to kill other people; kids who saw their parents beat each other. These kids are thirteen and fourteen years old! That marked a huge turning point with Circles. After that camping trip, kids started really respecting what Circles mean, and they started respecting each other."

ANGIE, ROCA STAFF

The Trauma of Violence

Our fundamental connectedness to one another makes us vulnerable to harm. As a species, human beings form groups to do what we need to do in order to survive in the world. As infants and children, we begin our lives wholly dependent on others. Within the first three months of life, babies smile when their parents coo at them and wrinkle up and howl when they see instead an angry face. Our capacity for empathy—to feel what others are feeling—is one of the primary means through which we forge bonds with each another. Biologically, we are hard-wired to form connection.

The core trust that develops from being well cared for by our first caretakers leads us to have faith in all human and spiritual relationships. According to psychiatrist Judith Herman, "The original experience of care makes it possible for human beings to envisage a world in which they belong, a world hospitable to human life. Basic trust is the foundation of belief in the continuity of life, the order of nature, and the transcendent order of the divine."[1]

Despite the power imbalance between adult and child, loving caretakers honor the individuality of the child. They use their power to nurture the child's developing sense of self. Resting upon a foundational sense of safety in the world, a well-cared-for child develops a core belief that the world is a meaningful and trustworthy place. From this secure base, the growing young person is able to make healthy attachments. He or she forms an identity and achieves competence, autonomy, and independence.

What, then, is trauma? Physically, it is blunt damage to the body; psychologically, it shocks our sense of self, security, and connection with others. Because our condition in the world is one of connectedness, we are harmed when others are abusive, neglectful, indifferent, or violent toward us or those around us.

With trauma comes the experience of helplessness and powerlessness. Trauma ruptures our faith in the independence and value of the self in the world. It also carries a profound betrayal of our trust in other human beings, whom we no longer assume to be trustworthy. Instead of supporting us, connections become a source of danger and harm. Our belief in the world as a place that is just and good begins to shatter.

A traumatic experience, by definition, leaves us feeling disempowered and disconnected.[2] At any age, trauma can disrupt our sense of meaning, faith in humanity, and belief in oneself. Victims of trauma "lose trust in themselves, in other people, and in God."[3] Many people are, in fact, deeply and repeatedly wounded by their relationships. For example, children who are uncared for or abused; people who experience and witness violence in their homes or communities; those who experience chronic humiliation and disrespect of themselves and their loved ones because of poverty and discrimination: all these people suffer severe and sometimes lifelong trauma.

> "If you've had sixteen years of adults not showing up but telling you they're gonna, or sixteen years of birthdays that nobody celebrated, this idea of sitting in Circle and trusting adults or other young people to show up for you when you are dealing with the hardest emotional stuff . . . that's like science fiction! For these kids, trusting the Circle feels like going on a trip to the moon."
>
> SAYRA, ROCA STAFF

The psychological pain that arises from trauma leads young people to protect themselves emotionally. One way to do this is to not allow any connections to develop. Withdrawal, dissociation, aggression, depression, shame: these are common reactions to chronic or acute psychological trauma. By cutting themselves off from emotions, young people hope to protect themselves from further harm. Drugs, alcohol, and sex serve to numb negative or unpleasant feelings, while anger and aggression push people away emotionally. These defenses mask their awareness of deeper, more painful feelings, such as abandonment, rejection, loss, and hurt.

> "Even when you don't want to, things are going to come up. Feelings are gonna come up . . . emotions.

Because something's wrong . . . you know? And when
you get to the root of where it is that the problems are
stemming from . . . they bring up emotions . . . and
it's hard. For a while, I just couldn't deal with the
Circles. . . . I was like, 'I can't do it. I'm not ready. I'm
not ready.'"

ROCA YOUTH

Isolation and aggression do not, however, bring healing. Instead,
these responses exacerbate trauma by creating conditions that
extend it further. When we cut ourselves off from our feelings,
we're less able to empathize with others. For this reason, children raised by traumatized parents are often abused or neglected
by them. Disconnected from their own feelings, the parents have
lost the ability to empathize with their children. The children
then grow up with the same emotionally shut-down patterns.
When young people insist that they "don't care" whom they hurt
or if they harm themselves, they are actually armoring their soft
and vulnerable selves. They're putting up shields that protect
them from feeling vulnerable to more harm than they've already
suffered.

Yet those who have lost their internal connections to their
feelings pose great danger to others, because they are psychologically unbridled from the restraints of empathy. They feel neither
love nor guilt. This absence of feeling—the state of mind we often
refer to as "cold-blooded" or "without remorse"—enables them to
harm others. James Gilligan, a psychiatrist who has specialized
in understanding violence, notes, "A lack of empathy sets anyone
on the path to violence."[4]

Gilligan asserts that all violence—even the most criminally
insane acts—originate from traumatic wounds to the core self.
The impulse to do violence arises from a buried sense of shame
and humiliation, which in turn comes from an absence of love
and care by others. To be treated badly is to experience an assault

on our sense of self and personhood. Damage to the self—to our sense of self-respect, self-esteem, and self-love—is experienced as an excruciating sense of shame. "To suffer the loss of love from others by being rejected or abandoned, assaulted or insulted, slighted or demeaned, humiliated or ridiculed, dishonored or disrespected is to be shamed by them."[5]

Committing violence is an attempt to restore pride by subjecting another person to the indignity of abuse. It is a futile attempt to transfer the shame of being unloved to another person. After the fleeting triumph of the moment, shameful feelings at the core of the self persist unchanged.

Just as isolation does not bring healing, so, too, violence fails to satisfy our core psychic need to be loved and respected. These needs are met not through dominating other human beings but through connecting with them. Cycles of violence are self-perpetuating, because they humiliate others, who then seek to reclaim their pride by degrading someone else. Gilligan argues that all violence is a struggle to restore pride in the face of a perceived insult or indignity. In this sense, he argues, all violence is really a struggle for justice.

But the kind of justice that seeks to balance relationships by inflicting further harm is only one way of thinking about justice. It is retributive justice that imposes punishments—harm for harm. It does not seek to repair or restore what was harmed or to address the underlying issues that may have driven a person to do violence in the first place. In other words, by inflicting more trauma in the form of punishment, the model fails to address the impact on the victim or to understand the earlier traumas that may have led to the offender's destructive behavior. Retributive justice is not a model of justice that ends violence; to the contrary, it keeps the cycle of violence going.

The model of justice that brings peace is a justice that heals. Healing justice attends both to the person who has been victimized by violence and to the one who is so "empathetically disabled" that he or she is willing to harm others. The journey toward healing for both victims and offenders aims to transform core feelings of shame and humiliation into a sense of dignity and respect. On the victim's side, those who have suffered trauma clearly need experiences of empowerment and re-connection—a journey best made in the company of a supportive community.

On the perpetrator's side, those who inflict trauma on others need experiences that restore their humanity as well. They need a healing journey that takes them away from shame and humiliation and toward honor and respect. For perpetrators, this journey starts with a full acknowledgment, however painful, of the moral and human consequences of doing violence. Acknowledging harm, in turn, leads offenders to the deeper journey of healing from traumas in their own past and eventually to "re-storying" who they really are as human beings. For both victims and offenders, the healing journey begins with telling and listening to each other's stories in community.

Sitting in the Fire: The Power of Witnessing

> "People desperately want to share their story."
>
> ANISHA, ROCA STAFF WORKER

The Circle can be a place for healing wounds that run deep in the fabric of a community. When people share their stories in a setting where they are respectfully heard, they and others begin to heal. Because this happens so often in Circles, it is said that all Circles involve healing to some degree. In our highly stratified society, not all people's stories are given equal value or equal voice. As a result, the opportunity to tell one's story in a space where others will respectfully listen is especially healing for those who have been silenced, isolated, neglected, and ignored. Those who have been chronically denied a place to tell their stories find that the experience of being heard with respect helps to repair

Roca youth

the foundation of dignity and self-worth that has been eroded by trauma, both event-based and systemic.

> "Healing to me is all about being able to express suffering or pain or even joy in the company of other people who are going to hold you. So I think every Circle can be healing. We did a talking Circle last week with young people, parents, and community members, and the question was, 'Where are you from?' It took a long time, because so many people are recent immigrants and wanted to share their stories.
>
> "Then we asked, 'What do you want to leave behind?' In answering this question, one person gave voice to something she had never told anyone and had been holding on to for so long, and she was able to do this in the company of so many people who were

supportive. She was able to release and let go, and
that to me was healing, both for her and for me, too."

VICTOR, ROCA STAFF

Kaethe Weingarten has coined the term "common shock" to refer
to the myriad of daily assaults that affect our mind, body, and
spirit.[6] These violations of people's integrity, autonomy, dignity,
worth, and self are disturbing for everyone. Not only those who
suffer the violations but also those who commit them and even
those who witness them feel the effects. Exposure to violence is
a form of common shock that pervades our society, but it is particularly intense in the lives of poor urban youth. The violence
they witness runs the gamut from the interpersonal violence of
a husband who beats his wife and children to the structural violence of a social system that denies basic human rights to whole
groups and classes of people.

We witness violations as victims, perpetrators, and bystanders. In each of these three roles—whether we are aware of it or
not—we are wounded by that exposure. In fact, research shows
that the impact of witnessing violence is nearly as traumatic for
us as being the direct victim of violence. Witnessing can also be
traumatic for professionals, such as police, social workers, health
care workers, teachers, and others, who are constantly exposed to
others' pain and suffering.

These daily assaults are endemic and epidemic in our society:
we witness them in the home, at work, on the street, and in the
images of our news and entertainment. Again, it is our basic connectedness in the world that makes us vulnerable. We *feel* the
pain of these violations. Even when they do not happen directly
to us, they threaten our sense of security, autonomy, and dignity,
precisely because we are, in fact, connected to others. We may
struggle to "turn off" our feelings of empathy or attempt to turn
away in order to protect ourselves, but our natural capacity for
empathy makes us open to the pain that others suffer.

The same connectedness that makes us vulnerable—and indeed subjects us to violations—also holds the key to healing us from trauma and violence. In the West, we view human beings as separate, isolated entities. Feelings such as hurt, pain, joy, or hope are considered the exclusive properties of individuals—I'm happy, she's sad, etc.—as if we create our emotional response to the world alone or in a vacuum. Furthermore, our culture teaches us to conceal many feelings on the assumption they are essentially private and often shameful. They are supposedly best relegated to the privacy of the home, the therapist's office, or the hidden recesses of our own hearts.

Yet we also know the power of sharing our feelings with others. Witnessing—witnessing what happens to others and having harms done to us witnessed by others—is a critical factor in both the experience of trauma and our capacity to recover from it. Witnessing works both ways: it has both the power to hurt and the power to heal. When we witness violence, we are affected, but *how* we witness violence determines its meaning for us. We have the power to transform its meaning and the impact of its subsequent trauma by *how* we witness it.

Specifically, the kind of witnessing that can transform trauma requires compassionate listening. We listen to another's experience of trauma with a clear moral stance that acknowledges the wrong done to the person. We do not have to take action to avenge, prevent further harm, or protect the person. We simply engage our humanity to "see" the injustice done to another. By contrast, we can witness without this compassion. We can witness without making a moral stance, or we can choose to look away. The power of compassionate witnessing lies in the moral connection that it forges with the person. It affirms his or her inherent dignity as a human being, despite having been treated otherwise by others.

Witnessing carries this power, because, in a sense, feelings are a collective experience. When we come together to express and share our feelings, we do so for the purpose of transforming those feelings. When our feelings stay locked inside us, they tend not to change. We tend to get "stuck." But when we open up and share our feelings with others, their feelings and ours begin to blend, meld, and flow in new directions. Almost imperceptibly, our feelings shift. This is the reason for rites of mourning, such as funerals or other collective processes that deal with grief, loss, or pain. Human communities have been dealing with suffering and loss for millennia. By coming together to bear witness to harm and to honor the wounds it has caused, a community engages its power to heal.

> "I was in a Circle with a young man who, for the first time in years, talked about his father's death and how much he missed his father—how painful it was that his father hadn't been able to see his first grandchild. He had been carrying that, and he found a space to be able to let it out and let it go. And just acknowledging that—acknowledging that pain and having other people acknowledge it—was very healing for him."
>
> ANISHA, ROCA STAFF

The Circle is a space where compassionate witnessing happens. It is a place where people can tell their stories and hear the stories others have to tell. By listening with compassion and without judgment, the Circle allows people to be witnesses for one another as well as for themselves. They hear their own pain in the stories of others. As a result, they are able to witness their own experiences from a different perspective when they share their stories with others.

The Circle is a place where we witness the stories of violence as victims, perpetrators, and bystanders. All three roles carry with them burdens of psychological pain. By sharing these burdens with the community, we begin the journey of relieving them. By witnessing violence and trauma with compassion, we engage the capacities inherent in communities to transform violence and trauma.

The Healing Power of Truth-Telling

> "Circle isn't about sitting around being happy. It's about sitting in the fire and holding each other in that."
>
> ANISHA, ROCA STAFF

An act of violence is a total denial of another person's autonomy, dignity, and existence. Violence is often described as "unspeakable," because it is a communicative act that denies the meaning and purpose of words. Violence obliterates the power of words to reach the heart and mind of another human being. Judith Herman, for example, notes that, "At the moment of trauma, the perspective of the victim counts for nothing."[7]

Because violence is a denial of voice, it is also a refusal to listen. Violence is the opposite of dialogue. In dialogue, people are allowed not only to express themselves and their view of reality but also to be heard and to have their views respected. In our society, structural violence renders whole communities mute and invisible for generations.

Violence is also shrouded and protected by silence. Families who witness atrocities and live through them generally never speak of these experiences with one another. In a community with many such families, the quiet is deafening.

> "My parents and some older folks would not talk about what happened in Cambodia. They just keep it to themselves. That's why they get crazy. Our family didn't talk about it. I don't talk to anybody. My father don't talk to anybody. Everybody just shut their mouth."
>
> SAROEUM, ROCA STAFF[8]

Among Central Americans, recent experiences with civil war, martial law, and trauma lead many to seek silence as a refuge. Not being able to talk about what happened is a frequent response to trauma.

> "If you see something, you get quiet. You don't say anything, 'cause that is where safety is, in the silence. The immediate response is to say nothing."
>
> SAYRA, ROCA STAFF

Yet silence perpetuates trauma. Trauma is transmitted from one generation to the next when survivors maintain a climate of oppressive muteness about terrible events. When the second or even third generations are denied the chance to serve as witnesses to their parents' and relatives' pain—when they cannot genuinely mourn with them the inestimable loss of lives, culture, way of life, homeland, and identity—the impact of the trauma lives on.

Yet, no matter how long a painful silence has prevailed, words still retain their power to transform violence. Words *are* mightier than the sword, because they offer the possibility of reconnecting and restoring. To speak the unspeakable in the presence of witnesses is to reclaim one's humanity. The slogan of the Truth and Reconciliation Commission (TRC) in South Africa is "The Truth Hurts, But Silence Kills." The Truth and Reconciliation Commission created an extraordinary space for compassionate witnessing and opened a space for twenty-two thousand victims and seven thousand perpetrators to tell their stories.[9]

By witnessing these stories—told in their own languages and in their own ways—the TRC and the people of South Africa honor the pain of the victims. More, they restore the victims to their rightful place of dignity and respect in the community. While the commission could not bring back loved ones or undo the past realities of torture or the legacies of physical damage, it could embrace the victims in the arms of the community in order to weep with them and comfort them, signaling that they were not alone with their suffering.

Words help to reclaim the moral principle that the violence was wrong, an evil, and a sin denounced by all. Violence flourishes in silence: looking away allows it to thrive. By publicly exposing the horror of violence in very personal and emotional ways, those who participated in the TRC hoped not only to help heal the wounds of trauma but also to prevent the perpetuation of violence.

For people to tell their stories of trauma—difficult stories about witnessing, experiencing, or perpetrating violence—others must be willing to listen. Voice depends on witnessing. Witnessing is not the same as identifying with what is expressed. To witness effectively does not mean that one must have had identical or similar experiences or feelings. On the contrary, our capacity to empathize with the pain of others whose experiences are different from our own is precisely why we are able to come together as communities. Our willingness to witness painful truths reveals the strength of our diversity. Through mutual witnessing, we help each other heal.

> "We are in a community that deals a lot with harm. People come from a place of war and witness a lot of crazy things in their country. So we know that in order to move forward as human beings, we must do a lot of healing, and we must use each other's strengths to do healing, because we can help each other heal. You know, if I'm Cambodian, I can't be talking to another Cambodian person, because they are going through the same things I'm going through, and there's no point. But sitting with other people, other ethnicities, gives us a leeway to share our stories and share the pain and share some of the things that deeply harm us or affect our lives."
>
> SAROEUM, ROCA STAFF

When we witness the pain and suffering of others, we call upon our humanity to recognize their pain, hear their cries for dignity, and acknowledge their feelings as common to our own. Regardless of our different experiences, we can create community and restore hope by showing support and solidarity. Violence is an act of disconnection. However, putting that wordless experience into a story and telling that story to others who open their hearts to the emotional truth of that narrative in all of its horror repossesses and redefines that experience. Through our power to communicate, whether in words or in other forms of expression, we create connection at the place of our most brokenness. Through this connection, we begin to heal.

> *Each person in the Circle was asked to draw a picture of a place where he or she felt safe. When the feather came to one young man, he stared down at his drawing. With downcast eyes, he held up the paper and began to explain the image he had drawn. It was a cemetery with a stick figure, himself, beside a tombstone. The tombstone bore the name of a friend killed by a bullet intended for him. This was where he felt safe; this was where he felt most at home. As he spoke, he wept.*

Society offers many reasons for refusing to hear the stories of young people like those who come to Roca. When charged with a crime, offenders are told by lawyers not to talk to anyone about what they did. Young people held in detention are instructed not to discuss their deeds with youth workers, who might be subpoenaed to testify against them in court. For those we label "violent" or "criminal," we withhold sympathy and deny them a venue for telling their stories. We don't want to hear why gang members commit crimes. We don't want to hear about the events in their lives that led to their current behavior. We have no empathy for the gang members who turn to graffiti and tattoos to express the depth of their grief. We see these only as symbols of anger and aggression, not as communications from the heart. We refuse to witness.

> "Tattooing is about cutting and bleeding and healing and carrying the mark of your grief until you die. And for young men in particular who don't have a place to give voice to that grief, it's very powerful. It's a very visceral way to grieve when you don't have other ways to do so. I am hoping to do more Circle work with young people around this. If a young person feels the need to memorialize in such a very permanent and personal way, can they be making other choices?"
>
> VICTIM ADVOCATE, DISTRICT ATTORNEY'S OFFICE

We also turn away from hearing the stories of victims within our society. We routinely rely on therapists and other professionals to deal with victimization, as if victims suffer from a rare form of pathology that only experts can understand. Young people who

Roca youth

have been abused or raped often confront layers of silence from parents and relatives. Denying their reality is a response that victims also hear from adults within social welfare and criminal justice systems. Sometimes professionals warn that if a victim discloses the abuse, the law will require that either the perpetrator or the victim be removed from the home, regardless of the victim's preferences.

If victims are referred to a professional in order to tell their story, an unintended message may be conveyed to the victim that talking about their experience of violence is unwelcome or inappropriate. When we worry—even with the best of intentions—that we are not trained to hear the stories of human suffering, we practice silence. And when we communicate a message of silence, we reinforce a sense of shame.

Learning the Language of Emotions

> "I think Circles have helped me find out that it's hard to deal with hard things—to deal with your past. It opens up things that I forgot, that I kind of suppressed. I guess you keep things down inside you, 'cause you didn't want to deal with them. . . . But in the Circles, you listen to others, and you say to yourself, 'Oh damn, I went through that, and it brings back some memories, and now I gotta go and deal with that. . . .'
>
> "So it's a constant dealing with myself. And you gotta keep at it. And you're gonna have some setbacks, but as long as you understand where you're at and who you can be, well, you keep going. . . . Circles have helped me figure that out and have understandings of where others come from, which is the key to relationships in life."
>
> ROCA YOUTH

To go deep in the Circle and share the feelings of vulnerability that lie right beneath the surface of anger and indifference, young people need to trust the Circle and feel emotionally safe in it. They must know that if they speak, others will truly listen without judgment or disrespect. To this end, the Circle has powerful protections for honoring the voice of all participants. By opening a uniquely egalitarian and respectful forum, the Circle becomes a place that young people trust enough to relax their tough exteriors to allow emotional healing to begin.

The Circle is also a place where everyone is encouraged to speak from the heart. To deal with trauma and the powerful negative emotions that lay hidden inside, we need to learn how to talk about emotions and acknowledge our feelings. For young people who have adapted to the harsh realities of their lives by shutting down, one of the core tasks of emotional healing is learning to speak the language of emotions.

> "Talking about feelings is hard. I think people are just scared. People are just scared of who they are. People just fear making themselves vulnerable or being looked at as weak. . . . But we're there for love. . . it's all love . . . when you are in a Circle. . . . And if you're not ready—if you have love issues or intimacy issues—it's gonna be kinda hard for you to sit there and listen to it, because it's deep. If you're not ready to deal with love, it's gonna be hard to kinda take it in. That's what scared me away. For a while, I didn't want to be involved, 'cause it's deep, and I wasn't at a place where I could handle that."
>
> ROCA YOUTH

To address this critical issue, Roca has adapted Circles to include the use of a powerful curriculum for developing emotional awareness and emotional literacy called "Houses of Healing."[10] Robin

Casarjian created this program for men and women incarcerated in our nation's prisons. But it has also made a profound difference in the emotional growth of the young people who come to Roca— youth who have both suffered high levels of violence and, in many cases, committed high levels of violence.

Most habitual, chronic violence goes on without those involved being aware of the emotions driving it, except perhaps the emotion of rage. Many inmates come from homes and communities where expressions of anger and violence are a way of life. Young people at Roca are also surrounded by expressions of rage: screaming, swearing, hitting, and beating.

They are less familiar, however, with the feelings that lie beneath the rage: the disappointment, loss, hurt, loneliness, humiliation, shame, and abandonment that arise from neglect and abuse. Like the adults in their lives, they shut themselves off from experiencing their vulnerability. They never had a community that felt safe enough to hold them in their sorrow and suffering.

Roca youth

To cope, they learned to be "tough"—to "not care" and to wear the mask of indifference.

"Our kids don't have people asking them about their feelings. In their lives, they don't have an adult saying, 'How are you doing today? How are you feeling?' So we practice it over and over and over again. The first couple of times, the kid tries. He will be, like, 'I'm fine, I'm straight. Nothing ever changes anyways. Okay, not a problem.' But on the fifth time, he is saying, 'Today, I had this and that happen, and the teacher did this, and I'm really pissed!' That's huge, 'cause my kids, when they're pissed, they shoot you or punch each other. Talking about feelings has got to be something that we practice."

DEPARTMENT OF YOUTH SERVICES STAFF WORKER

Houses of Healing (HOH) is a self-help course designed to help men and women in prisons become aware of their emotions. The program helps them do this by helping them explore the events and relationships that shaped their behavior and the feelings that led to their conduct. HOH offers new ways to re-story oneself. People learn to take responsibility for their actions and to engage with the world peacefully. To support this shift, the course teaches meditation, spiritual practices, and daily mindfulness. Collaborating with the young people at Roca, Robin and Bethany Casarjian adapted the HOH curriculum to be relevant for youth at risk and developed a book and curriculum called *Power Source*.[11] These curricula are combined with the practice of sitting in Circle.

Both curricula recognize that anger is a powerful but ultimately superficial emotion. It masks deeper, more painful feelings of grief, loss, and hurt. The overall program offers young people a chance to practice emotional awareness and to consciously choose how they will react or respond to negative situations. These are core elements of becoming emotionally literate.

> "When we first brought about fifteen guys from the street together in Circle to do Houses of Healing, I just figured they would not share anything, really, and it would be a hard time for us to get through to them. But I guess I underestimated them. They created a culture and called each other 'The Brothers' Keepers,' 'cause it's all young men. They came up with their own little ritual in the beginning of every Circle. We all stand up in Circle, and they step in and say, 'Am I my brother's keeper? Yes, I am.' People will say, 'So what are your commitments as a fellow Brother's Keeper?' And they will repeat some of the guidelines: 'I will be respectful' and everything else. It's been amazing how they take charge. We are the keepers, but we never felt like we 'kept' those Circles. That's been amazing."
>
> VICHEY, ROCA STAFF

The Circle offers a safe place to explore the tender regions of the heart. Slowly, young people ease into using the language of emotions in a space that is safe enough for them to give voice to all of their feelings. Learning to speak about one's emotions in the company of others is a difficult journey. But honest dialogue about the painful realities of violence—interpersonal and structural—is the most hopeful path away from cycles of violence.

> "At this point in my life, I know how to deal with my emotions more. . . . I don't react to anger as I used to. . . . Recently, someone came and attacked me. My first reaction before would have been . . . you know . . . [shakes head]. . . but now I have an under-

standing about where that person might have come from. I give them the benefit of the doubt. I don't want to react, 'cause I really want to be this way anyway, so if I react out of my anger and things, then I'm not gonna be who I really want to be. I think Circles helped me find that out."

ROCA YOUTH

Speaking the truth about one's own wrongdoing in the presence of others is profound. Yet, in order to acknowledge the real impact of our actions on other people, we need to be able to empathize with them. This capacity for empathy begins with a willingness to feel and acknowledge one's own pain.

"We had a Circle about grief and death, and some kids feel like they are someone who's really a bad ass out on the street, so if they talk about something sensitive, they may lose respect, or someone out on the street might think, 'Oh, that's a weak spot.' But in the Circle, if they see someone else cry, they are like, 'Wow, you cry?' And they're like, 'Well, I cry too,' and I can share my experience and let that out as well, rather than keeping it inside and holding it in and thinking that nobody else has those feelings too."

DEPARTMENT OF YOUTH SERVICES STAFF WORKER

Developing Empathy: Becoming Aware of the Impact on Others

In a detention facility, a young woman was making life miserable for the thirty or so other young women by keeping them up screaming. Recognizing the woman had some mental health issues, the staff struggled to quiet her, but with little success. Night after night, she disturbed the entire unit with bouts of screaming. The staff decided to hold a Circle to give the other young women a chance to tell her how her behavior was affecting them. In the Circle, each person spoke, and one of the girls shared, "You know, I was gang-raped, and listening to your screams night after night brings it all back to me. Every time you scream, it brings it all right back to me." The young woman was deeply moved by this revelation, and to the astonishment of the staff, the behavior stopped. In the words of the staff director, "It was awesome."

The staff at the detention facility had tried different strategies to get this young woman to stop this distressing behavior. They had used the stick of punishment and the carrot of rewards by imposing "consequences" for her conduct. But like all forms of punishment, these contrived consequences were part of an artificial control system imposed by the adults in the detention facility. They were not the *actual* consequences of her behavior. By contrast, during the Circle, this young woman learned about the *real* impact of her screaming on others in the facility. Learning how her behavior was affecting others, combined with her capacity to empathize with them, induced her to change.

> "Fewer of us may think ourselves capable of witnessing a perpetrator with an open heart and mind. Yet, perpetrators are profoundly in need of such witnessing if they are to develop the capacity first to honestly reflect on their injurious actions and later to witness those they have harmed. In many communities and societies, however, there are no means by which perpetrators can be assisted to repent and change. They are frozen as evildoers."
>
> KAETHE WEINGARTEN[12]

Accountability and healing are two sides of one coin. They work best together, each increasing our capacities for the other. These two complementary processes blossom in an environment of support that offers both respect and acceptance to someone in deep personal struggle. Those who have harmed others need to be able to empathize with them in order to acknowledge the full impact of their behavior on them: this is what accountability involves. To empathize, though, those in personal struggle with their behavior must be emotionally healthy enough to endure painful feelings: this is what healing involves.

Young people who have walled off their feelings are unable to empathize. An overwhelming sense of shame from their own pain has led them to close their hearts for self-protection. The journey to accountability is, therefore, also a journey of healing from past wounds. As young people learn to read the language of their own emotions, they become aware of the emotions of others. Slowly, they open themselves to connection. As they do, they open themselves to feeling how they may have hurt others. This

Roca youth

painful acknowledgment is both the mark of healing and the start of genuine accountability.

> "Perpetrators must be given ways to take responsibility for what they have done, express remorse, and perform acts of apology, restitution, and restoration so that they can live in the world no longer as perpetrators. We need to develop practices and language to match, so that people are not forever doomed to think of themselves as perpetrators or be regarded as such by others."
>
> KAETHE WEINGARTEN[13]

A Place to Grieve

"When Desi died, everyone from Project Victory decided to go to room 233 and have a Circle about death and about appreciating people before they die, and how you say 'I love you' to somebody before they die and not while they are lying in a casket. After the funeral, they came straight to Roca. 'Sayra, Angie, we want a Circle. We want to run a Circle. We want to keep a Circle. Give us the candle and a space.' Sayra was, like, 'Okay, but you need to have an adult there,' so they said, 'Angie, can you come?' I said, 'Okay, I'll go with you guys.'

"They ran the Circle. They put Desi's picture on the floor, and they put all these sacred things. . . . One of the girls brought a special thing that was hers because her mother passed away, and they used that as the talking piece. It was really good. And these kids are thirteen . . . running the Circle. They did guidelines on a flip chart with markers, different colors. They

burned sage. They took Desi's picture and put the
sage around it and smudged it. Then they started
with an opening and a closing. . . . I didn't have to do
anything. . . . They just did it."

ANGIE, ROCA STAFF

When it comes to sharing difficult and painful experiences, the
dominant culture does not offer us many rituals for using the
healing power of words to restore hope and meaning. Coming together to grieve and mourn is one of the few rituals we have for
witnessing emotional pain in our culture. At times of loss, communities gather around those suffering in order to share their
pain and to offer comfort through their presence and support.

Yet, while we are still alive, we often fail to use these rituals to
honor people's lives and the grief we carry—to fully acknowledge
the impact of our many losses or to express our emotional pain. As
a culture, we are unpracticed and unskilled in expressing grief or
using the language of comfort, even for traumatic events such as
illness or death that affect us all. Those who want to witness another's pain often feel awkward, helpless, or afraid that they will not
respond in a helpful manner. Those in pain are often fearful of their
own emotions and mask their pain with drugs. Just as we turn to
experts to manage the bodies of the sick, dying, and dead as part
of their professional duties, so too do we seek out professionals to
help us deal with emotional pain. Ordinary people—as most of us
see ourselves—doubt our capacities to listen to our own pain or to
the suffering of others without specialized assistance or training.

Circles, however, are a space where emotional support flows
naturally. Participants support those in pain, and they support
each other in their efforts to give support. In times of grief—
and there have been many—the young people at Roca have
quickly gravitated toward the Circle as a place to be when they
experience loss.

*These thirteen-year-old girls knew they needed to come
together to deal with the loss of Desi, a thirteen-year-old boy
struck down in front of the center in a hit-and-run accident.
The funeral and wake organized by adults did not meet their
needs, since the adults gathered in silence and then retreated
to the solace of alcohol to cope with the pain. Rather than
seeking refuge through rage, isolation, drink, or drugs, these
young people sought a form of relief that is ancient and common to all societies. They came together as a community to
mourn the loss of a beloved.*

Acknowledging losses and mourning them are essential to interrupting cycles of violence. Suppressing grief is a short-term reaction to violence. Indeed, it is part of the emotional shock that
marks the very first phase of grieving. But getting stuck in this
phase through a long-term refusal to fully mourn contributes to
cycles of revenge and retaliation. People who suffer loss but are
unsupported in their mourning may become filled with anger and
rage—another early phase of grieving. These powerful but unpro-
cessed emotions fuel a desire to lash out to seek relief. Numbed
by the habitual use of alcohol and drugs, the pain of the loss remains buried, but it is still very much alive, driving behavior and
affecting relationships.

Being in Circle interrupts this cycle of pain. The values of Circle
encourage participants to learn how to speak from the heart. Even
though the emotional pathways for doing so are often blocked by
layers of hurt and anger, the Circle space persists in inviting participants to share some of their own vulnerabilities. Through this
sharing, people who are isolated begin, however slowly, to find
connection, solace in one another, and the start of healing. People
can speak the unspeakable or simply release their grief.

Whereas grieving in solitude often feels overwhelming, if not
intolerable, grieving in the company of others who empathize
with us and honor our pain is healing. Being able to sit with pain,

to acknowledge it, and to accept its reality frees us from the crippling effects of carrying pain in silence. By holding an outer space where pain can be expressed, Circles support the formation of an inner space for healing. This inner healing enables us to embrace accountability and to make the needed changes in our lives and communities.

> "Once you are able to let go, I think you get a sense of healing. By your sharing, you are being heard, and you don't feel lonely no more. You feel like the whole world waits and hears and listens to what you got to say, and that's really, really good."
>
> VICHEY, ROCA STAFF

Honoring Harm: A Gift of Healing

What does it mean to "honor harm"? In her book *Trauma and Recovery*, Judith Herman describes the role of the therapist as an ally in the recovery process—someone who acknowledges the experience of the survivor of violence. As an ally to recovery, the therapist is willing to listen to the story fully, hear it in all its horrific details, and accept it. The role is one of solidarity with the victim. From a moral perspective, it is neither detached nor neutral. The witness is clear that what happened to the person was wrong, that they did not deserve such treatment, that they are valued as a human being, and that they have, indeed, been deeply hurt.

Honoring harm also involves a willingness to open oneself to empathizing with suffering. The witness does not turn away but has the courage and compassion to stay and listen. It is not about fixing the hurt or curing it. It is simply about being present with pain and offering the solace of empathetic awareness, which builds connection. Through the act of compassionate witnessing, the community as listener restores to the person some of the psychic losses that the trauma caused.

> "The solidarity of a group provides the strongest pro-
> tection against terror and despair, and the strongest
> antidote to traumatic experience. Trauma isolates;
> the group re-creates a sense of belonging. Trauma
> shames and stigmatizes; the group bears witness and
> affirms. Trauma degrades the victim; the group exalts
> her. Trauma dehumanizes the victim; the group
> restores her humanity."
>
> JUDITH HERMAN[14]

Communities have the power to rebuild each of the three beliefs shattered by violence: safety, compassion, and dignity. But they need to exercise this power. Communities can develop their capacity to bear witness to the painful realities of trauma and to offer solace to victims. Sadly, contemporary society largely ignores these powerful roles and responsibilities. As a result, the ability of communities to honor and support those who have suffered has atrophied.

Young people often pay the price. Those who carry enormous secrets about the violence in their lives feel chronically shamed and isolated. The ongoing violence they experience demonstrates the truth of South Africa's TRC slogan. For these young people, speaking the truth may be painful, but silence is worse: it can be deadly.

Circles offer communities a means to reclaim their powers. Through its rituals and values, the Circle opens a space for the community to bear witness to violence—past and present. Telling one's story in community is a gift both to oneself and to others. Being in a space that is safe enough to speak one's truth in the presence of others who are truly listening carries great healing power. Those in pain and the community heal and grow stronger together.

> "There's something about pain and loss that they
> really need to talk and just be in there in that state.

Keeping Circles is hard, especially when you have someone who just shared that they were raped when they were four years old. As a keeper, it's really difficult to figure out the next question when you have something planned out, and it doesn't go to where it is supposed to go. That happens all the time. When I have somebody say something really profound and start crying, I'll stand up and hug them. Then I'll say, let's go another round without saying anything. I'll just pass the feather around again. Sometimes we just need to take a deep breath, and other times I'll say, 'This was good. I'm really proud of you guys. . . . Every Circle is different, but this is one of the best Circles we've ever had. I feel really privileged that you guys trust me enough to share.' The challenging part is just knowing exactly when to stop or when it is the right time to stop or when it is the right time to keep going or to move on."

ANGIE, ROCA STAFF

By offering their own experiences, participants express generosity to others in the Circle. Telling the story of being a victim of violence, of losing a loved one to illness, or of losing one's social position is a precious gift to those listening, who may recognize their own suffering and shame. By sharing what is most painful, storytellers cultivate a generosity, because then the healing that goes on in the Circle touches far deeper levels. The experience is valuable not only to those in pain but to everyone present as well.

"I just remember sitting in a Circle where I was gonna talk about my dad. And a few people were talking about their dads, like yeah, their father wasn't there either, and that sort of made it okay for me to share mine, 'cause, wow, I could relate to that. I'm going

through the same thing she's going through. I feel
like that too, and that makes it okay, and I feel like,
'Wow, I want to share my stuff.'"

VICHEY, ROCA STAFF

At the same time, the storytellers are themselves vindicated by
the moral support that comes from others in the Circle. Their suffering and its impact on their lives are recognized and respected.
Thus, the benefits of healing within the Circle are mutual: both
those who tell their stories and those who listen gain from the
sharing. The outcome is that the community strengthens its capacity to care for itself by providing this vital function.

"I think people heal when they feel like, through their
suffering or their story, someone else might benefit
or someone else may learn something or someone
heard it. I think that in itself can be very healing.
There have been Circles where adults have disclosed
sexual abuse as a child but have come to enough
places in their lives where they share it in a way
that is about helping someone else, and that's very
healing."

ANISHA, ROCA STAFF

Honoring harm is about honoring the humanity within us all. It
is about recognizing that the degradation and humiliation that
violence spawns—the rejection, hurt, and shame it produces—
does not define who we are, either as individuals, as a community,
or as a species. Honoring harm is about seeing each other as the
sacred and valued persons we truly are.

"See, to me, you can talk about Circles on two different levels. One is the level where it's a process: it's behavioral, it's equal, it's democratic participation, it's

consensus building. . . . There's that level of it. Then there's this other level of it, which, to me, for me, is really about . . . how we create sacred spaces where we hold each other sacred. When we can recognize the sacred in each other, we're in a sacred space."

ANISHA, ROCA STAFF

Finally, honoring harm is about realizing the power we have to "show up" for ourselves and each other. This is something we can do. Perhaps more important than all other lessons, the experience of sitting with each other in the place of our most brokenness reveals the fundamental and awesome wholeness of the community. Violence may be unspeakable, but love is heard loud and clear in the words, gestures, and simple presence of brilliantly ordinary human beings who come together for the sake of one another.

"To me, the potential of this simple little thing, this Circle, to invite healing for people with so much pain and suffering—including myself sometimes—is so extraordinary. It's so simple, it's dumb. But my gosh, this is within our reach. We can't undo these things, but we can have healing, and we can have forgiveness."

MOLLY, ROCA'S EXECUTIVE DIRECTOR

CHAPTER SEVEN

Opening the Heart within Systems

"If blame is being passed out, no one can elude taking their share. The parents whose neglect caused their child to be taken into care, the extended family and the community who failed to become involved, all of the professionals—public health workers, social workers, teachers, police officers, probation officers, and, yes, judges—who have done our jobs in the same old way. All of us must share the blame for the endless parade of children through our hands and into dysfunctional lives. By now, we should know better. We must do much better."

BARRY STUART[1]

Roca has shared the Circle with dozens of professionals from agencies and systems whose work impacts the lives of disadvantaged youth and families. Now, several organizations, both large and small, have adopted the Circle. As its use spreads, the Circle's influence is radiating far beyond the small city of Chelsea.

The Circle is not a form of magic; it is a way of coming together that is profoundly different from the patterns that now exist in our social institutions. Sitting in Circle gently alters the quality of relationships among people. For this reason, when Circles start to be used in seemingly inflexible bureaucratic organizations, they initiate—quietly and almost invisibly—a profound process of change.

Social workers, probation officers, teachers, guidance counselors, and police officers were among the first people invited to Circle trainings at Roca. Word of mouth brought more people from these organizations to Roca. Within months of the first Circle training, peacemaking Circles began to appear within juvenile day-reporting centers, detention facilities, social service offices, home visits, staff meetings, and local area classrooms. In some organizations, gentle pressure from supervisors or senior staff encouraged people to participate. Some managers even insisted that staff members learn about Circles. Others simply gave enthusiastic staff members permission to hold them, leaving those less interested untouched by the process.

Based as it is on core values of equality, connectedness, and respect, the peacemaking Circle is more than just another strategy added to the organizational toolbox. It introduces profound change, which flows from the most basic features of Circles. For example, by giving voice to all participants—including young people, clients, and the community—the Circle challenges the standard assumptions of hierarchy based on credentials, status, or power. Also, by encouraging people to share not only their mental and technical knowledge but also their feelings, hopes, fears, and dreams, sitting in Circle unsettles norms of professionalism and expertise. Moreover, because Circles bring together different people in a different way to talk about different things, they help create new relationships between co-workers, clients, supervisors, colleagues, and community. People often come away from a Circle with fresh ideas about what is possible.

With ongoing use, Circles initiate currents of change just below the placid surface of organizational life. Professionals come to "see" their clients, the community, co-workers, as well as themselves through a different lens. This new way of seeing invites people to think, speak, and act differently. Preceding any formal changes in structures, policies, or procedures, then, are these less

Roca youth

visible—but perhaps more significant—shifts in perceptions and habits of the heart among those who participate in Circles.

Championing the Circle

Major change processes require champions—and committed ones at that. Individuals who have felt moved to introduce the Circle within their own organizations have faced enormous challenges. Pressed for time and resources, people in work environments tend to be set in their routines and resistant to change. Circle advocates have needed considerable commitment to endorse a process that many view as quirky, impractical, unnecessary, time consuming, and unprofessional. When ridicule and skepticism about its value arise, they have needed courage to continue to support the process. Circle champions persist, because they sense the power of the Circle and are convinced of its potential value to the organization. They understand how much Circles can help an organization fulfill its mission with young people and families.

The director of a secure DYS detention facility, for example, was among the first staff from the DYS to be sent to a Circle training at Roca. Unfamiliar with Circles or the concept of restorative justice, this DYS administrator had no idea why she was asked to go to a place called Roca for four days. Her initial reaction was negative. The rituals of the Circle struck her as "a throw-back to the sixties." She failed to see how a process like this could be useful in a secure detention facility where supervision, security, and control were high priorities.

> "My concept of restorative justice and Circles was almost nonexistent. I'm on the conservative end of the department. I think in terms of schedules, rules. Things are usually black and white as far as policies go, more of a military nature. By the second day of the training, I could not see the Circle working in detention at all."
>
> DEPARTMENT OF YOUTH SERVICES ADMINISTRATOR

Even more disturbing for her was a serious conflict that arose early in the training over the guideline of confidentiality. As mandated reporters, certain state personnel are legally required to report information disclosed to them to law enforcement and other agencies for criminal investigation. The DYS administrator and other DYS staff explained that they could not set aside this legal obligation in order to preserve confidentiality within the Circle.

The reaction from community people, especially young people, to this position was intensely emotional. They explained that they could not feel safe or develop a sense of trust without the promise of confidentiality.

The stalemate lasted for hours, as the feather went round and round without resolution. As it went, it unearthed deep feelings of mistrust and hostility within the community toward the juvenile justice system. The DYS administrator and other professionals felt attacked, disrespected, and misunderstood in their steadfast refusal to agree to maintain confidentiality in the Circle.

> "When we were doing the guidelines for the Circle, confidentiality came up. Well, I said I have no solution, because I will not agree to that, and therefore it's never gonna work in detention. . . . It just can't. Treatment, maybe, but never detention. Then we had a break, thank god, because I had a migraine headache by then. I was just so miserable. . . . I can't even tell you. I thought this is awful. I'll be very honest with you, I didn't want to go back for the last two days. If it were up to me, I would have left.
>
> So I'm standing on the corner with Harold having a cigarette with my coffee, and in my sarcastic tone, I said, 'Oh, this is going great,' and he said, 'Yes, it is going great.' And he was serious! I said, 'How could you say that?' And he said, 'Just let the process work. You'll see, a solution will come.' Thank god I didn't go home the first or second day, because I would have said, 'waste of time.'"
>
> DYS ADMINISTRATOR

What this administrator did not realize is that Circles are uniquely able to "hold" conflict in a constructive way. By the end of the four days, the director felt safe enough in the Circle to acknowledge the validity of the community's perspective and to express how hurt and misunderstood she felt by their attitude toward her. Each side was able to see the truth of the other.

Although the specific issue was never resolved, a solution was found. A relationship of respect formed between this systems professional and the community based on an understanding that they all genuinely cared for young people. Far more significant than gaining a short-term compromise or pragmatic resolution about confidentiality, the Circle revealed the capacity for genuine dialogue. Each side began to truly hear the perspective of the other.

> "We came to an understanding really that you can agree to disagree. But what was really important was for me to tell them something. There were people in that Circle who were anti-system and that bothered me. Like they have no idea who I am. I consider myself to be—or was at one time—anti-system too, especially growing up. My purpose for coming into the department was because I didn't like some of the things going on in the community, and I figured I would go in and change some of those things. I believed that was possible to some degree. So I challenged people at that Circle, 'You people who are anti-system, if you don't like the system, why don't you join it and change it?' I mean I really do believe that."
>
> DYS ADMINISTRATOR

This relationship opened possibilities for collaboration in the months and years that followed. Within six months, the DYS administrator asked Roca to conduct two trainings at the detention facility. She wanted to begin using peacemaking Circles for behavioral issues, education, and substance abuse programming with the young women. Despite their vastly different approaches, the security-minded detention director trusted Roca to help bring Circles to her facility, both for staff and for the young women who were incarcerated there. Because the Circle helped everyone focus on what they had in common—the goal to help young people thrive—they were able to respect the profoundly different ways that each of them worked to achieve this goal.

"By the third day, I thought, well, maybe this Circle is good, maybe if we have a small number of kids, just the good kids. But then I learned that you gotta be inclusive of everyone in Circle, so I'm like, 'Oh my god, it's not gonna work, there's just no way.' Then by the final night, I thought, 'Okay, I'll take the risk, because I'm tired of seeing the same kids over and over and over again. They go home, they come back, and it's just a revolving door.'

"I got excited because there were a few kids in the Circle training who were really hardened, like those I see at DYS too. At the beginning of the four days, I thought to myself, 'They're gonna get nothing out of this and neither am I.' But little by little, I saw them pushing themselves to engage. I think they felt safe in the Circle and that said something to me, because that's one of the problems we have in detention: you don't have enough time for kids to feel safe. The Circle seemed to expedite the way they feel connection and are willing to talk. So that was one of the things that impressed me, observing these kids. No one was pushing them saying you must talk, but the whole concept of Circles is very welcoming to them. They feel comfortable to just say things. I thought that was extremely impressive."

DYS ADMINISTRATOR

Another early champion of the Circle was a local area director at the Department of Social Services. After attending a single Circle at Roca, she was instantly drawn to the process. She believed that the Circle offered social workers a way to genuinely communicate with families and to help them strengthen their own systems of support within the community. In her view, the Circle offered a form of communication that empowers families. It gives them a greater sense of control as well as respect in their relationship with social workers. She also suspected that sitting in Circle would enhance the families' capacity to communicate among themselves and to explore how they could take more active and constructive roles in addressing their problems. She immediately asked to send members of her staff to learn about Circles.

> "In my mind, Circles provide a process for us to do
> our work. It gives us a method to sit down and talk
> to a family. It gives us a way to engage that family to
> do the kinds of things the department is hoping we'll
> do, like strengthen a family, and second, communi-
> cate with that family. The Circle also leaves the family
> with something of value, so they can depend on
> themselves. I saw the Circle offering some options to
> a family for managing their own business after we've
> left their lives."
>
> DEPARTMENT OF SOCIAL SERVICES AREA DIRECTOR

The former commissioner of the Department of Social Services in Massachusetts also became a champion after attending a Circle training at Roca. He attended the training during the months before he became commissioner. Based on a long-standing con-nection to the city of Chelsea, he heard people talk about "this Circle thing" and became intrigued by their enthusiastic reports. At a personal level, he was grappling with the difficult decision of whether to accept the post as commissioner of a massive and troubled social service system.

> "I did my first Circles just before I became the commissioner. It was actually the stage where I was pondering whether or not to accept the position of commissioner of DSS. Molly invited me to come and do the Circle training at Roca, but she didn't know at the time that I had been offered the job of commissioner of child welfare."
>
> FORMER DSS COMMISSIONER

In a poor community like Chelsea, social services, court, police, and correctional authorities are a constant presence in the lives of most young people. Not surprisingly, the role of social services in the community came up in the Circle. The soon-to-be commissioner sat anonymously within the Circle, realizing that this was a golden opportunity for him to hear the perspective of the community without anyone knowing he had any connection to the agency. He braced himself for hearing the inevitable horror stories of mistakes, anger, and frustration.

> "Somebody brought up DSS, and there came to be a discussion about the role of the department in the city of Chelsea. The department is probably more active in Chelsea than in any other community in the state, because Chelsea is the poorest city in the state, and there is a significant correlation between poverty and child welfare. So it is very, very active in Chelsea. I realized that this was my last chance to be a fly on the wall in a conversation about the department, because nobody had any idea that I had any connection to DSS. I thought, 'Oh boy, get ready,

now you are about to hear every ugly story about the department.'

"What I heard was really fascinating. I heard people say, 'Sometimes they drop the ball and sometimes they get it wrong, and when they do, they really screw things up.' But—and this started with some of the older folks—people started saying, 'Hey, did you know what it was like before they were here?' A consensus emerged in the Circle that, 'We wish they'd do better, but boy, are they important to the life of this community!'

"Did they think the department was flawless? No. But did they believe that the work was deeply important? Yes. And I tell this story to social workers at the department, because I say, 'You ought to know that in the community most impacted by our work, they know that the department has saved kids' lives, but they were calling for the department to do better. There is a recognition that the task is hugely difficult, and we need to do it better.'"

FORMER DSS COMMISSIONER

Hearing the voice of the community inspired him to take on the challenging position of commissioner for this agency. In this capacity, he became a champion for bringing Circles into the work of the department.

The Need for Profound Change

Large public systems, such as the DSS and the DYS, routinely fail to meet the needs of poor youth. We know that the problems of poor youth are rooted in systemic issues—the immense inequities and injustices of the global economy. For decades, inner-city communities have endured a steady decline of decent jobs. They have lost the very jobs that once provided the economic foundation for both families and the institutions of community life.

This once stable economic base has been replaced by a heavily lopsided labor market. A few highly paid jobs for skilled professionals perch atop a massive number of low-paying service jobs. Unemployment, gangs, drugs, crime, and violence concentrate in communities that are increasingly isolated economically. The more affluent residents have fled to the suburbs or to gentrified sections of the city and walled themselves off from those "left behind" through private security systems.

Into the breach have stepped our public, private, and nonprofit social service organizations. These service groups are charged with addressing the mounting chaos of communities struggling with economic and usually racial oppression. Social workers, mental health counselors, doctors, urban planners, social scientists, and other professionals are hired to examine the problems, assess needs, and create services aimed at "fixing" these problems. Residents within communities such as Chelsea become clients of these professionals and recipients of their services.

Without question, the people and especially the youth in these communities are in crisis and need help. Yet something is fundamentally wrong with this approach. Despite good intentions and a massive investment of resources, these service systems fail to empower the people they serve. They do not cultivate the respect, care, connection, empowerment, and self-sufficiency that individuals, families, and communities need to thrive.[2] Instead, community members are reduced to being passive consumers of services. They come to depend on the expertise of professionals, rather than on the homegrown support of family, friends, neighbors, or local associations, such as churches or clubs. Ironically, over time, the primary skill that many people pass on to their children is a convoluted knowledge of how to "work" a system that sees them largely as deficient individuals.

The inadequacy of this approach is plain to see in the behavior of young people, who almost always run away from—not back to—the home placements that social services provide. Professional systems of service delivery are no substitute for strong and healthy communities. They simply cannot provide the relationships of love, respect, connection, trust, and mutual responsibility that healthy communities draw on to support community members through hard times. Beyond delivering services, we need to engage and rebuild communities.

The commissioner of child welfare heard communities ask systems to "do better" in addressing the complex challenges of their youth and families. The question is, how? If systems keep doing their jobs in the "same old way," we should expect to see the same old results. To create a world where all young people belong, everyone—including systems—must change. This means we most likely need to reinvent the way professionals do their jobs: from the judge in the courtroom, the teacher in the classroom, the social worker in the office to the police officer on the street. Just as young people who wish to leave the street must learn to walk a long, hard road of behavioral change, so, too, must the systems that intend to strengthen the internal assets of families and communities become organizations that know how to change.

Peter Senge, an organizational theorist, draws a distinction between a problem-solving approach to organizational change rooted in deficits and a creative approach to change rooted in vision. Problem-solving tends to be backward looking; it relies on existing technologies, habits, and structures to make a liability or problem go away. If the problem is a shortage of staff, the solution is to acquire more resources; if the problem is a lack of access to services, then the focus is on finding ways to increase access. Problem-solving returns us to a previously conceived state or assumed status quo.

Creativity, by contrast, fundamentally looks forward; it draws on our ability to imagine what does not yet exist. Approaching organizational change creatively draws on a vision of how things might be. Roca holds a vision of a world where all young people have a sense of belonging and value. The tension between this passionate vision, rooted in cherished values, and a brutally honest accounting of the current state of affairs—a society where "troublesome" youth are routinely shunted aside, excluded, rejected, neglected, and ultimately discarded—generates the creative energy to figure out how to do better. This kind of aspiration challenges large organizations to fundamentally transform the values, procedures, policies, and practices by which they operate. In other words, it calls for a kind of organizational change that is not trivial but profound.

Learning Organizational Change

> "These young people deserve for us to be our best
> all the time, and if we're not growing and changing,
> we're not doing our best. Something about the Circle
> invites us as an organization to go there. Something
> about Circles lets us practice organizational learning
> and development. The Circle taught us some kind of
> habit, practice, safety, comfort, and courage to ask,
> 'Are we really doing what we say we are doing?'"
>
> MOLLY, ROCA'S EXECUTIVE DIRECTOR

In order to sustain effective work with young people over time, Roca became an organization that knows how to "learn" and how to "change." Change processes in organizations are similar to the dynamics of change in individuals. Like individuals, organizations need a vision for the future; they need to reflect on their core values, achieve clarity about their purpose, and design effective action toward their goals. They must learn to take a hard look at themselves and examine the truth about what they have achieved in order to discover how it may—or may not—measure up to what they say they would like to do.

Roca youth

At Roca, a vision of a world where all young people belong and thrive motivates organizational learning. In 1999, because Roca was operating as a learning organization, it was able to recognize the value of peacemaking Circles for its particular vision, mission, and values. Adopting the peacemaking Circle, in turn, has initiated even more profound changes within the organization. Roca found the Circle to be a powerful space to continue the practice of organizational learning and development. The Circle helped to transform the organization, enabling it to make the changes necessary to achieve its next level of purpose.

Indeed, bringing Circles into the organizational world of systems often prompts an interest in organizational change, even when the Circles were not introduced for this purpose. Circles are a form of practice: people sit differently, without a table or desk facing one another; no leader makes decisions; everyone has an equal voice; and each person must wait as the talking piece makes its way around the group. The physical layout of the Circle reduces distraction and concentrates attention. There are no papers to hide behind, no seats in the back, no side conversations, and no notes passed. It is not possible to multi-task in Circle: one is either speaking or listening. Although Circles have keepers, keepers do not direct the process and are not decision-makers. Making decisions is consensual, which involves everyone and takes time and patience.

Sitting in Circle inevitably raises profound questions at all levels of the organization. As Molly says, something about Circles encourages people to ask hard questions about what they're doing: What vision of the future drives the work of social services or juvenile corrections? What is the agency's mission? Do staff members agree on this vision and mission? Which values are important in their work with young people or families? Are these values evident in the organization's actual work?

Typically, management and disciplinary practices contradict Circle values of respect and equity, and this discrepancy can generate palpable tensions within the organization. Do supervisors listen to subordinates? Do they treat them with respect, compassion, or justice? These are some of the hard questions that arise when Circles open a space within systems for organizational self-reflection, learning, and development.

> "In Circle, we realized that staff had different notions about our work, and so we found out that, even though we do the same job, we had different thoughts about the job, and then we had to live with those differences on the floor. Now, if we're confused about the way that we're going, what are you thinking the little souls must feel? They're gonna be ten times more confused. So we used the Circle to develop a vision and values statement for our facility."
>
> DYS FACILITY DIRECTOR

In most large organizations, these questions are rarely explored. If they are discussed in any official way, usually only the discussions held by senior management count. Rarely do these discussions include front-line staff, janitors, clients, or community members.

Circles, by contrast, work like a container where new ways of thinking, acting, and feeling have the time and space to incubate. Participants are free from the pressures of routine, hierarchy, practicality, crisis, or impatience. As a container, Circles are designed to hold voices normally excluded from discussions, both from outside the organization—such as clients or young people—and from within the organization.

Perhaps more important, the Circle liberates voices that have been silenced within each individual. They create a space where people can share emotional and spiritual truths not often brought into the discursive space of everyday organizational life. As a result, Circles help us bring all parts of ourselves to the work of our organizations.

Organizational Change Begins with Listening

Enormous barriers often prevent genuine collaboration and communication between systems professionals and the communities they serve. Community members and clients do not feel on equal footing with the professionals who hold considerable power over their lives. They do not feel respected or heard when they must deal with someone operating in the official role of social worker or judge. They are afraid to speak. The organization's jargon is foreign to them, and, given the lopsided power structure of the relationship, they seldom feel that their opinions will be valued equally. They do not trust one another; they fear one another.

> "Many times as I sit through foster care reviews in our system and other kinds of meetings, we talk at the families or we talk to the families, but we don't talk with the families or visit with them. Many times, you will hear a parent who is in a lot of pain really saying, 'You're not listening to me.' To me, the Circle is the equalization of everybody who is sitting there. That I

think is the most valuable, because it hopefully begins
to build our respect for the parent or parents. Too, it
helps to build some self-esteem for that parent to be
an equal participant. And I think it makes us listen."

DSS AREA DIRECTOR

Circles open avenues of communication between those who are
marginalized and silenced and those who hold positions of power
and privilege. Because the Circle empowers the voices of those
who are otherwise powerless or silent, it offers vital feedback to
systems professionals about their work and the impact of their
decisions. Although most people learn best from experience, organizational decision-makers rarely experience the real-life consequences of their most significant decisions. Hearing from the
community changes that. It offers new insights about the short-
and long-term impact of the decisions they make about other
people's lives and the value of the intervention or services they
provide.

> "There was a young woman whose family was
> involved with the department, and I had the op-
> portunity to listen to what she had to say about
> how she felt about the department. After hearing
> her, I believe we need to hear from the family and
> individuals—what the impact is from their perspec-
> tive, not just what *we* think the impact is. We need to
> know that what we do in this agency has an impact
> not just for the moment but for the long term. How
> important it is for us to hear what other people have
> to say about the kind of work that we do!"

DSS DEPUTY AREA DIRECTOR

Circles reduce the barriers between families and communities
on one side and system-paid professionals on the other, because

professionals "take off their professional hats" and share their experiences as human beings. When people come together in Circle, the experience usually humanizes them for each other. Those from the system see whole people instead of deficit-bearing clients, and those from the community see whole people who are more like themselves—beyond their job responsibilities. As stereotypes and prejudices relax on both sides, people gradually are able to talk and share advice without as many layers of mistrust, negative perceptions, and judgments overlaying their interactions.

> "Because you enter into the Circle process without titles, and you enter into it with your own experiences, you now have a conversation between human beings, instead of 'I'm the director of community services, and you're the parent who's got a kid in our system, which means you're a no-good parent.' Those kinds of perceptions are taken away, and it really allows parents to hear us in a whole different way."
>
> METRO DYS AREA DIRECTOR

In addition to using Circles as a better way to communicate with clients, organizations are finding that Circles provide a different way for staff members to listen to one another. Staff meetings are sometimes the first place where people experiment with the Circle process. Those from the organization who attend a Circle training bring back an understanding of Circles as a way to increase communication and encourage staff members to express themselves openly and honestly.

> "I think the Circle does the same thing for staff that it does for families. It makes people equal. People have to listen to everybody, and I think they get an opportunity to express what they are thinking or feeling. In

the bureaucracy, there is the hierarchy, and whether you intend to build it in or not, there is this fear of authority. Because the bureaucracy doesn't cultivate speaking up, the bureaucracy cultivates grumbling. It's the same with us middle managers: we are not talking to the assistant commissioners and commissioners. . . . we're not speaking up.

"I think the Circle provides a forum where you as a supervisor can get your message out, and where they, the staff, can get heard. The Circle allows people to be themselves, but you also have to participate. You can't kind of sit in the back row, kind of be there, and then get up and leave. You have to participate."

DSS DEPUTY AREA DIRECTOR

Circles slow things down, which is both beneficial and challenging for many people in the work environment. Compared to the frenetic pace of dialogue, interaction, and decision-making in most workplaces, the Circle feels glacial in movement. Yet slowing down cultivates patience and enhances the skill of listening. Because participants feel no pressure to interject comments or respond, they become more aware of the act of listening and more appreciative of its benefits.

"We're so used to this quick, fast-paced society. Everything happens, and it's question–answer, 'Let's get this done.' Circles are not like that; they are completely different, and I think that is what people have the most difficulty with."

DSS SOCIAL WORKER

"I've heard that folks are sometimes put off by how long it takes to go around the Circle, and it does take time, but then I think it depends on what it means to

you to listen to people. Some people don't have that
patience and are constantly on the go, but the Circle
slows you down. It gives you an opportunity not only
to deal with your thoughts but also to listen to other
people."

DSS SOCIAL WORKER

One senior-level administrator realized that staff members rarely
slow down long enough to reflect on the value of their work. The
only time this happens is when they are out of the office attending conferences or workshops, but these creative time-outs have
little impact on the organization's culture and practices. By using
the Circle process within the organization's internal routine, staff
members give themselves a chance "to step out of the river" and
think about the meaning of their work.

"You hear people talk about going to a conference
that you go to, and it's as if it were a timeout. All you
are doing is talking about work with other people
who are in the same business, but somehow it is so
incredibly refreshing to actually have the opportunity
to step out of the river and talk about it. In some
ways, I think that's part of the value of the Circle:
it allows you to call a timeout and talk about what's
going on, as opposed to just answering your pager
and keeping things moving."

DYS DEPUTY COMMISSIONER

Circles are also a place to address conflicts and problems. In one
office, a series of Circles was designed to develop procedures for
transferring youth between facilities and community programs.
When the Circles actually convened, however, they focused almost entirely on the underlying conflict between the staff in the
facilities and the staff in the community programs. People as-

sumed that simply creating protocols would resolve the perpetual conflict between these two departments. Yet, as with the issue of confidentiality, being able to share the *reasons* for their conflicting perspectives provided a deeper solution. It reduced the mistrust and misunderstanding that constantly led to the negative interactions between the two departments in the first place. Once they understood each other better, agreeing on the actual protocols was a piece of cake.

"We struggle as an agency to help facilities understand community-based programs and vice versa. Talk about strife between vendors and state workers: well, we have strife between state workers! We've done a number of different things to try to address this conflict, and nothing has worked.

"Addressing this conflict wasn't even our intention in these Circles. Our intention was to develop a consensus about certain protocols for revocation, but everybody brought up frustrations created either by community staff or by facility staff. And because they were able to express some of the stuff that happens in the facilities and some of the stuff that happens in community, people were able to put things into context.

"It finally broke down some of the walls that existed between community and facilities. Before, they would automatically think, 'Oh, someone hasn't called me back, because they just don't call me back.' They just felt that—just that that person didn't call me back, and it becomes personal. In the Circles—I think we did seven or eight of them over a period of months—people became more mindful of what other people's jobs entailed and all that was going on. The facility people were like, 'Wow, I never even thought of that,' and they were much more empathetic to the plight of the work that those folks were doing in the community.

"And the community people, well, the fact is that our numbers are so high, and we've had a lot of overcrowding in the units at the facilities. Community people know it, but they're not being reminded of it, 'cause it's not in their face every day, whereas for the facility people, it's in their face all day, every day. They have staff being forced to do double-double shifts, because there's not enough staff and they have too many kids, and they have to have a certain amount of staff ratio.

"So expressing those kinds of things allowed people to really come to a middle ground and think, 'Gee, I've got to be mindful of those things when I'm having these phone conversations.' And they were talking a lot more among each other. And there were a lot more commonalities that they agreed to. They all wanted the same thing for kids, you know, but they got so caught up in the personal stuff—and became bitter with each other about these things—that they've allowed them to snowball, until they sort of lost track of what the goal was."

DYS AREA DIRECTOR

Learning to Be Whole at Work

By its very nature, the Circle challenges many norms of behavior in professional work settings. The workplace is often seen as a place that is about mental and technical expertise rather than emotional exchanges or personal sharing. A judge reflecting on his experience with Circle remarked, "I could come to work at this courthouse for years, and no one would know a thing about me."

Essencia Latina in performance

In Circles, however, people participate as full human beings. They speak from the heart about what matters to them, share stories about themselves and their families, and, when they feel moved, express emotions. Circles offer employees a place to talk about their emotions, both in terms of their relationship to their work and to their lives outside the workplace. Co-workers are often shocked at how little they know about the people they have worked with side by side, sometimes for decades.

Some find the Circle practice of speaking from one's own experiences and hence of getting personal one of the most challenging aspects of Circles. People are aware of status differences and are afraid of exposing themselves in the work environment: What will the boss think? What will my subordinates think? Can I afford to share my experiences or how I experience my life, or is it safer to stay hidden and invisible? For others, the Circle offers an opportunity to establish different boundaries within the workplace—boundaries that allow space for personal revelations.

Ultimately, the increased understanding that follows tends to increase productivity.

> "People have barriers they put up: 'I only want you to know what I think you need to know at work.' Other times, you'd like to have a relationship with people at work, but then you feel like, 'Well, he works for me, and if I share this with him, then he may think this.' But in Circle, people just feel comfortable. And it's okay to say, 'When I was a little kid, Christmas was horrible' or 'Birthdays weren't always that great.' So it allows us to get to know each other on a different level. So far, that factor has been a positive experience."
>
> DYS FACILITY DIRECTOR

Those who work with youth and families in crisis have a particular need to pay attention to emotions within workplaces. According to the DSS commissioner, "It's hard to say that we care for kids and then to say that the moral and emotional development of our staff doesn't matter." The stress of the work demands high levels of emotional fortitude, especially since emotions can be endlessly drained by the overwhelming day-to-day impact of what youth and families go through. Professional staff who witness trauma on a daily basis may themselves be functioning in a state of chronic secondary trauma. Unless this ongoing trauma is addressed in some healing, restorative way, it can lead to coping behaviors that are dysfunctional for both the professionals and their clients.

> "Particularly in this business, this is an issue, 'cause we've got our own baggage, and because we sustain secondary and tertiary trauma day after day. The police department, they have psychologists who are

assigned to do nothing but trauma work with the officers—grief work, personal issues . . . whatever. They're required to participate, and I'd love to be able to have that for our staff too, 'cause if our folks are healthier, our kids and their families are going to be healthier too."

DYS DIRECTOR

The Circle has proven itself a valuable tool for staff to examine their work, their emotional states, and their attitudes toward work. Staff members in social services and youth corrections are sometimes ambivalent about their roles. They get frustrated and depressed by the enormity of the social problems they face as well as emotionally exhausted by the trauma and pain they witness on a daily basis. Circles open a space for the staff to talk about their mission and discuss some of the underlying tensions inherent in how the juvenile justice systems or social services work.

"It's funny. In some ways, we're sort of caught between two worlds. We are in many ways a correctional organization. Some things are just non-negotiable or somebody's gonna get hurt: we do restraints, we make arrests, we do some unpleasant things. And I think actually one of the things for staff is that those are sort of the ugly things, . . . and they make it easy for an organization like this to get ugly. When Molly uses the terms 'doing it from sort of a good place,' well, if I have to take you to the floor because you are going to hurt yourself or others, there are two ways to come at that. We can do it from a good place, or what we don't want are people who sort of take it as a challenge and slam you to the floor and try to show you who's in charge. That's the kind of culture we are trying to avoid.

"Plus, we have people who do some terrible stuff: we have kids who try to commit suicide, kids that do commit suicide, kids who are killed in the community—that kind of stuff can get to you after a while. So for staff, Circle is a way to figure out what it is that we are trying to do here and how we are trying to do it. You know, kind of check in to make sure we are all coming at this from the same attitude, that our intentions are good. It's a place for staff to talk about some of the things that they do and some of the things they experience."

DYS DEPUTY COMMISSIONER

The commissioner of social services for the state believes that the Circle process is a powerful tool. It gives staff members an opportunity to heal themselves, which in turn opens possibilities for them to be more creative, optimistic, and overall positive about their work.

"A key issue in the department is that our workers are constantly exposed to trauma, and they have been provided with no resources to manage that trauma or their responses to the trauma. . . . They are dealing with the deepest, darkest places of the world. . . . And if we are to close the gap between what the vast majority of our workers long to be doing and what they actually do, it's gotta be by giving them immensely more of both substantive and moral support.

"So the Circles struck me immediately as one way for workers to get this support. . . . Circles provide a wonderful setting for healing work for people who are in pain and who together share a common pain. So what I'm interested in is how Circles can be used to of-

fer everyone an opportunity to make a place—a place
that is organizationally supported by the systems—
for them to process their emotional experiences."

FORMER DSS COMMISSIONER

The Art of Leading Change

The cumulative impact of all these "seeds of change" suggests that
bringing Circles into the workplace is about much more than adding another tool to the organizational menu. Far from being an
overnight solution or a quick fix, Circles invite deep transformation. Yet such change is what both organizations and the individuals within them resist. Even when the benefits of change clearly
outweigh the negatives, most efforts toward change within organizations lack the drive and endurance to persist long enough
for change to become natural. Thus, before changes reach the tip-
ping point where positive rewards keep the momentum going,
the change process requires consistent support from individuals
who are prepared to stay committed over the long haul.

"The idea of learning organizations is that we all deal
with the problem that people are vastly resistant.
There is stunningly little real recognition that change
is painful and that there is no learning without pain.
Therefore, an organization has to be prepared to deal
with this and constantly say, 'Let's keep asking the
question and keep learning.' Any change in practice
will never occur without an evolution. So sustaining
change is part of what is important, and workshops
don't work. They just don't work. People love them
and desperately want to change their practice, but
they don't change their practice."

FORMER DSS COMMISSIONER

Leading profound change within organizations—and hence coping with the inevitable resistance to change—calls for the art of
leadership, rather than the science of management. Management
is about maintaining control over people's actions in the interests
of order and consistency. Managers need to know where they are
going, so they can assess when they get there.

While command-and-control management can sometimes be
effective in ensuring that specific rules or policies are followed,
profound change in what people think, believe, and value requires
that people choose to learn freely—of their own desire. Leaders
can create opportunities for this kind of learning, and they can
model learning by making the choice to do it themselves, but they
cannot make people learn something if they don't want to.

Any process of organizational learning involves a long-term
investment of time and resources. Learning about Circles and
then integrating them with organizational life are no different.
Both the organization and individual participants must keep up
their commitment to the Circle work. A typical Circle requires
two to three hours of sustained conversation. Attending a Circle
training at Roca requires four continuous days away from the
normal duties at the office. Beyond these practical logistics, the
Circle itself challenges the fast-paced, crisis-driven norm of most
workplace environments. It often generates complaints that the
Circle is "wasting time" or "inefficient." Resisting this kind of
feedback and staying the course require a calm and consistent
faith that the long-term value of Circles will outweigh the short-
term costs.

> "I thought if I start pushing Circles for this purpose,
> it's going to be seen as this slightly eccentric commis-
> sioner's hobbyhorse. And part of the problem is the
> constant churning in organizations like this, where
> every commissioner has 'their thing,' and I've been
> anxious to avoid this. . . . Circles require a willing

suspension of certain prohibitions within the organizational culture, which is why I thought it'd be better
to help support and nurture the use of Circles, rather
than try and impose it. It doesn't work to try and
impose it. You have to want to do it."

FORMER DSS COMMISSIONER

In a leadership-centered culture, everyone cultivates his or her
own leadership skills and respects the leadership skills of others.
Establishing such a culture is the ultimate act of leadership. As
Peter Senge observes, "'Organizations are webs of participation[;] . . . change the participation and you change the organization.'"[3] Circles definitely "change the participation." They bring
different people together in a different way to have a different
kind of conversation. These conversations are designed to reduce
the social distances created by age, position, class, race, gender,
life experience, and so forth.

By setting aside social divisions, Circles open spaces for leadership to spread. In the open, democratic dynamics that Circles
create, powerful systems actors begin to share leadership with
those who are typically disempowered, both in their own organizations and in the community. With wider participation come all
sorts of possibilities for authentic partnerships. The organization
and the community start interacting in new ways.

This brings us back to one of the hidden lessons of the Circle,
namely, that "It's about us." As people display their commitment
to Circle values by practicing them personally and promoting policies that uphold them in the organization, they demonstrate the
source of the Circle's power for change: the power of people to be
our own leaders in transformation. After all, value-based changes
take root within the hearts and minds of individuals as well as in
their relationships. This is where real change starts.

Understanding that real change comes from the people of an
organization much more than from formal policies and procedures

inspires people to appreciate the kind of leadership that Circles foster. If the only one you really get to change is yourself, then leaders lead by modeling the change they wish to see, rather than by handing down rules or policies. Leaders provide opportunities for each person to choose a path of change, and they support people as they explore possible changes. When people examine their values and consider their commitments and obligations to an organization's work—which Circles invite them to do—they engage in the kind of shared reflection that makes deep, constructive change possible.

> "I think we need to become almost like one kind of giant mentoring organization. That's the thing I find kind of funny about us engaging in efforts to bring in mentors. Staff members are with these guys three shifts, twenty four hours a day, seven days a week, and sometimes for a year. These people ought to be mentors—every single one of them: the cook ought to be a mentor! And there are people here who are very good, very good. . . . I'm just not sure we have consciously adopted this as a culture.
>
> "Circles are a way to introduce that kind of thinking in people's head. What are we doing here? If it is the way that you carry yourself, then you are working when you wake people up in the morning. There is a way to do that, a way to restrain people, a way to do all the mundane things you do that keeps you safe and the kids safe, but also communicates to that kid all of the qualities you want to communicate to a kid: the respect and the feeling that the kid is valuable. Circles are a way to bring this out in people. And again, you can't put that in a memo . . . and you can't bring people in for a two-hour training on

how to be a good person. . . . Circles are truly about
staff development."

DYS DEPUTY COMMISSIONER

Gateways to Change

It is difficult to see large-scale organizations as living systems
that need to grow and evolve. Their impersonal, hierarchical
charts that map out cascading pyramids of roles and responsibilities seem to defy evolution. Nonetheless, the structure of organizations is neither divinely ordained nor immutable. In truth,
organizations are human inventions. They are creative solutions
to past challenges. As such, they are neither fixed in place nor
finished once and for all. On the contrary, given the world we
now face, yesterday's solutions are quite inadequate to respond
to today's challenges, much less tomorrow's. We know this, and
yet we cling to organizational patterns that we inherited from
previous eras.

Creative change does not happen out of the blue. There is an
art and even a science of it. Like learning, creativity requires an
intentional letting go, a willingness to look beyond usual constraints and to absorb new understandings. If organizations continue to rely on existing procedures, information, and modes of
decision-making, then we can anticipate that future outcomes
will be more of the same. When the goal is to solve a problem,
looking to the past for solutions that have worked makes sense.
But when the goal is to create change, we need to find ways to
open ourselves to new ideas, insights, and possibilities.

Circles offer a powerful space for doing this. Organizations
that have embraced the Circle process in any significant way—and
more and more are now doing so—have embarked on incredible
journeys of learning and creativity. Inventing a child welfare organization that truly supports families and communities, for example, cannot be the work of one person, no matter how brilliant or

powerful. Neither can a juvenile corrections agency that values all young people, regardless of how difficult or "damaged" they may be, emerge as the brainchild of a single charismatic leader. Deep changes such as these simply cannot be mandated from above.

Instead, change must draw on the willingness, commitment, and creativity of each person involved. Organizations must find ways of doing the work of change together. Only then can they utilize the immense gifts of leadership, knowledge, and creativity that exist not only within the organizations themselves but also beyond them—within the communities they serve. There is no place like Circles for practicing this radical inclusivity or for engaging in learning and change that is this profound.

CHAPTER EIGHT

Bringing Justice Home

"Justice is a funny word. When you live in a place where that word is used all the time, it can mean many things. Mostly I think it means 'us versus them': someone wins and someone loses, justice as domination. We think of justice as 'just us.'"

VICHEY, ROCA STAFF

One of the great gifts of Circles is that they help us recognize the power we hold collectively to make choices about how we live together. Through the scientific and social technologies of the industrial age, we have extended the power of our minds to dominate nature and to transcend the physical limitations of our own puny biology. These technologies enable us, for example, to walk on the moon, fly around the globe, communicate instantly across time and space, or even peel an orange at our kitchen table that was picked from a tree halfway around the world. Yet at the start of the twenty-first century, we are stymied by how to extend the power of our hearts to respect and embrace all of humanity or to care for the whole of living creation. We have created awesome powers of destruction that threaten the very existence of the planet, and yet we fail to meet the most basic needs of all our children.

Circles offer a social technology that extends the intelligent and compassionate power of the human heart. The oldest symbol for "mind" within Chinese culture is a drawing of the heart.

Within the Circle, people practice seeing with the heart, speaking from the heart, and listening with the heart. Circles create a space in which all voices can be heard and participants can recognize shared values despite social differences. In this way, Circles open opportunities for a sense of "we" to emerge—a "we" that draws on the creativity of all people, not just those who sit at the top of a social hierarchy. Circles help us connect with what is most universal within ourselves and therefore with what we have in common with others. The result is a sense of unity that represents a profound shift in our mental and emotional framework.

> "In Circle, you don't come as anybody else but yourself. Police officers or mayors in the community don't get to come as police or mayors, really, but just as concerned persons. 'Cause all the time we come to meet, we are separated from one another by titles; we come as this or that. But in Circle, I don't care if you are this or that, you sort of leave that outside the door and really bring yourself, and it's really about bonding and getting to know each other."
>
> VICHEY, ROCA STAFF

Circles help participants listen with respect and actively seek solutions, instead of assigning blame. Being in Circle encourages people to take shared responsibility for constructive action. It does not demand that others fix a problem. Participants focus on shared values, common purposes, and connections among people, groups, and organizations. The Circle experience cultivates a sense of ourselves as a "we"—as a community. This emerging sense of "we" honors our interdependence as well as our collective destiny.

> "When the 'they's' go away and the 'we' shows up, people's awareness and capabilities change. . . . When

> people who are actually creating a system start to
> see themselves as the source of their problems, they
> invariably discover a new capacity to create results
> they truly desire. . . . if 'we' are creating the problems
> we have now, then we can also create something
> different."
>
> SENGE ET AL.[1]

What does the Circle have to do with justice? Our professional-ized society often fragments our common life into specialized spheres. Not surprisingly, then, our thinking about justice gets broken into different arenas as well. We use the language of pro-cedural or criminal justice to talk about responding to violations of the law. We use the language of democratization or transitional justice to talk about creating fair political structures. And we rely on ideas such as distributive justice, economic justice, racial jus-tice, or social justice to talk about the inequalities in our society.

But are these realms really separate from one another? The Reverend Dr. Martin Luther King Jr. observed that injustice anywhere is a threat to justice everywhere. In our ordinary lives, justice is holistic and fundamentally indivisible. Injustice in one realm gives rise to injustice in another. It is obviously valuable to apply the Circle as an alternative process within the criminal jus-tice system. But the question we ask here is deeper: Is the Circle a path toward creating more just societies?

The Wisdom of the Blocks

In Roca's second year of using the peacemaking Circle, a visitor to the center brought a strange new opening to a Circle train-ing. In the center, he placed a dozen or so pieces of smooth drift-wood. His instructions were that each person would have a turn at composing the driftwood into whatever form he or she wished. When each person was done, it would be time to pass the feather

Roca youth

on to the next person, who could add, alter, or simply leave the composition as is. The process was to be conducted in complete silence with only the haunting sounds of windpipes floating in the room.

Within months, this peaceful exercise evolved into a raucous and contentious method for demonstrating something important about the power of Circle in community. The haunting music was dropped, and the driftwood replaced by a bucket of brightly colored blocks. Everything else about the exercise remained the same. At the beginning, participants are told that they can build, alter, or leave what is there alone, and when they have no further changes to make, they can simply pass the feather along. Each person has a turn when the feather comes to him or her and passes when he or she is done. The entire activity is performed in silence.

What teachings may be found in a simple game of building blocks? Each time, in its own way and time, Circle participants discover the wisdom of the blocks, occasionally with ease, but more often with intense discomfort and struggle.

The exercise begins cautiously as people collaboratively build teetering towers and sprawling structures in the center of the Circle. As the feather travels round and round, the building becomes more playful as people expand on the possibilities. In silence, people create, pick apart, knock down, and rebuild the colorful mass in the center of the Circle.

As minutes turn to hours, however, undercurrents of resentment, surprise, rowdiness, aggression, silliness, and frustration surface in the body language and facial expressions of participants. People glance nervously at the keepers, wondering what the true purpose of the game is and when it will end. Someone usually decides to take control and uses his or her turn to pointedly return the blocks to their container. Another person inevitably uses a turn to defiantly dump the blocks out and start building again. Feet shift, sighs escape, and eyes roll, as the feather continues around the Circle. Time and again, the blocks are put away, and time again, they are taken out. Sometimes they are placed outside the Circle or even removed from the room altogether. Invariably, someone retrieves them, dumps them out, and begins building all over again. Exasperation and confusion fill the room.

The exercise sometimes lasts for hours before the Circle participants learn the "hidden" lesson of how to end this game. People struggle to get others to stop playing by hiding the blocks or forcibly removing the box of blocks from the room. Blocks are thrown, cradled, hidden, stolen, even placed at people's feet or on their heads, as the group moves leaderless through uncharted terrain. In one Circle, participants from a correctional facility tried to end the game by placing handcuffs on the wrists of the keepers!

Eventually, however, each person in the Circle remembers the original instructions and realizes that the block game will end when each person chooses to stop playing and simply passes the feather. For this to happen, each person must first become aware of the choice and then make it for themselves.

Discussing what just happened after the exercise brings to light a powerful set of lessons about Circles and the unique nature of leadership that goes with them. During much of the game, people use their turn to persuade or communicate to others what they want them to do. Much of their energy is spent trying to get others to stop playing, even though they themselves have not stopped. The keepers, on the other hand, have been patiently passing the feather for hours. When people finally realize that the only behavior they truly control is their own, they experience a revelation. This is the wisdom of the blocks: "The only one you really get to change is yourself."

> "I think that what continues to be so powerful about the lessons of these Circles is . . . the personal change piece, right? I mean, it's great that you learn that you can do things in community, heal, and talk about hard things . . . all those important things. But you really have to change yourself, right? Or what is the point? And since you can only change yourself, you really aren't getting it until you are doing that."
>
> MOLLY, ROCA'S EXECUTIVE DIRECTOR

The blocks hold other lessons as well. During the debriefing, people talk about the different meanings they read into what other people do with the blocks. Without the opportunity to speak, each person developed their own theory about the intentions and meaning of others' behavior. These assumptions were charged with emotions: people felt accepted or rejected; they perceived aggression or imagined alliances; they felt either thwarted or supported by others. One of the powerful lessons of the blocks is how quickly we make assumptions about other people's actions without really knowing what is in their minds or checking in with them to ask what their intentions really are.

A third powerful lesson from the block exercise is how different our needs are. Some participants were ready to stop after two or three rounds, while others wanted to keep playing for hours. Whose needs are more important? In community, if one person wishes to keep playing, should the game continue? What do patience and tolerance mean? How aware are we of the needs of others? Do we care about meeting their needs? What does it mean to come to agreement? In the absence of a structure of hierarchy and control, how do we take concerted action? In a truly egalitarian structure, how do we come to a consensus that meets the desires and needs of everyone?

These questions have no answers, but the dilemmas raised by the block exercise are the dilemmas we face as we create change in our communities. How important are the needs of a young person who delights in the blocks and wants to persist? Can the community wait until everyone is ready to stop playing? Who decides when enough is enough? Who really controls other people's behavior and actions? When we create something together, are we so focused on telling others what they need to do that we forget what we need to do? And what do we really know about the intentions and meanings of other people's behavior if we have not asked them to explain it to us?

Sitting in Circle has transformed how Roca works with systems, city agencies, organizations, and other community members. Because of the Circle, Roca began to behave differently. Roca staff members made a conscious effort to stop assuming that people who disagreed with them had harmful intentions and instead asked questions and listened to the responses. Roca stopped trying to make others do what Roca wanted them to do and focused instead on fulfilling its own responsibility to show up for young people "in a good way." Roca took seriously the lesson that the only one you really get to change is yourself. And because Roca changed, it created space for others to change as well.

> "The Circle invited us to be better as an organization for young people—that's the first, most powerful lesson. Forget all the other stuff—engaging institutions, changing the world, systemic change, forget it! The Circle keeps inviting us to be better: What do you need to do to show up for these young people? The Circle is a space that made us listen, figure out what's important, figure out how to work with people in a way that works for them, and stay in those relationships, because young people need us to do that whether they like us or not. What do we need to do to partner with the police? How do we have to show up? Forget what they have to do. What do we have to do? In the end, it's our responsibility and our privilege, really."
>
> MOLLY, ROCA'S EXECUTIVE DIRECTOR

Moving from Blame to Responsibility

> "At Roca, we had been organizing one group of people to fight another group of people, and we've been very good at that. We were so furious, so righteous, so angry at how people were treating young people and the community, especially the poor community, that we became negative as well. So the Circles shifted us. We realized we need everybody to be at the table. We don't need them to be on our side, but we need them to be there."
>
> SAROEUM, ROCA STAFF

Like most grassroots social justice organizations that serve youth, Roca has been a fierce advocate for young people with schools, police, city agencies, and social services. Roca's staff has testified and lobbied on behalf of young people. They have organized and led feisty coalitions to defend or promote certain issues within the community. At times, their community organizing has placed Roca in opposition to other agencies and organizations. For example, Roca conducted a highly contentious campaign to distribute condoms within the high school. While Roca accomplished its goal, their campaign left a legacy of resentment, misunderstanding, and division within the community.

> "There were issues that Roca was fighting for on behalf of their clients that seemed to run counter to the goals of the community. There were also some questions about Roca's motives behind their actions. I think that one way that Roca has changed is that now they tend to look for other ways of getting around an issue before they have to come up with a fight. Fifteen years ago, it was fight first and ask questions later."
>
> CHELSEA CITY OFFICIAL

During those years, many people in the community made assumptions about Roca's actions and developed theories about what they were doing. Some believed that Roca harbored gang members in the center. Others believed that they condoned and supported illegal behavior. Many thought that they held values that were vastly different from their own. In the very first Circle training at Roca, some of the participants did a role-play that depicted a conflict on the street between youth and several members of the Chelsea police department. The scenario was hypothetical, but the patterns of behavior were familiar to everyone present. The emotions that the role-play generated were real.

"Within seconds, all my ideals about being a peacemaker went right out the window, and I understood
that I had been living by 'I am right and you are
wrong,' perpetuating the very thing we wanted to
change. At that moment, I realized that the Circle
was going to ask a lot more of me than just sitting in
a circle."

MOLLY, ROCA'S EXECUTIVE DIRECTOR

The practice of sitting in Circle changed how Roca showed up in
the community. Sitting in Circle led Roca to a deeper awareness
of what it really means to collaborate with other agencies in the
community. Was Roca respectful of those with whom they disagreed? What assumptions were they making about the intentions of the district attorneys or the police? Did collaboration
mean it was necessary to agree? Most important, what was best
for young people and the community? Was the adversarial approach to community organizing the best way to build the community necessary to support young people?

"Often when agencies bring people together to try
and build a collaboration, it's about people trying to
impose their views. People say, 'Well, we are all gonna
come together and collaborate, and then I'm gonna
tell you why what I'm doing is right, and you should
see the light and do things my way.'"

VICTIM WITNESS ADVOCATE, DISTRICT ATTORNEY'S OFFICE

Because Roca changed, they created space for others to change
too. By modeling a different way of being in partnership with others, Roca demonstrated through their conduct and behavior a better and more effective way to be. They paid attention to their own
responsibility to "show up in a good way," which inspired others
to do the same. Whatever the issue or project, they came with an

Anisha Chablani, Roca staff

attitude shaped by Circle values: an open mind and an open heart. In doing so, they did not make the prejudgments typical of their former approach—judgments about who was on the "right" side of the issue and who needed to change in order to see the issue correctly. Instead, they came to help and to ask for help.

The more they adopted this stance, which was supported by sitting in Circle, the more they saw people differently. Before, they used to automatically fight with the police, juvenile corrections, or conservative politicians. Now they saw these people not as the caricatures they had created out of their own assumptions and interpretations, but as who they claimed to be. They learned to genuinely ask what their intentions, assumptions, and goals were, and then they learned to genuinely listen to their responses.

Building Relationships That Last

> "The fundamental insight of 20th century physics
> has yet to penetrate the social world, namely, that
> relationships are more important than things."
>
> SENGE ET.AL[2]

When the director of a secure detention facility sat in Circle and heard the angry reactions of the community to the disagreement over confidentiality, her strongest impulse was to leave the Circle. Others in the Circle might have seen this as the best outcome as well. In polarized conflicts, the urge is for each side to retreat to its camp and resolve to carry on its own agenda without the obstacle posed by those with whom they disagree. The result of this "solution" is a divided world. Each party remains attached to the righteousness of its own perspective, unaware of different vantage points. With this solution, we see only our disagreements with others and easily come to believe that that is all there is to see.

By creating a space for genuine dialogue, Circles help to transform the energy of disagreement, so it becomes constructive rather than destructive. In the Circle with the DYS administrator and the community, both sides were able to explain their perspectives, and both sides listened to the other's concerns. There was profound truth in the community's history of betrayal and enormous value in their desire to control their own lives. Yet there was also profound truth in the DYS administrator's passionate commitment to keep young people safe by following legal rules. Learning to see another's point of view without denying the validity of one's own perspective forges relationships that last.

More important than a pragmatic compromise on a particular issue, then, is the dialogue that reveals the underlying reasons for divergent positions. When we share these reasons in a space where we genuinely listen to one another, we begin to discover the values, commitments, experiences, and desires that we hold in common. At the end of the day, what we have in common is far greater than the comparatively trivial issues that would otherwise drive us apart.

> "From Roca I've learned that sometimes the people you presume are your adversaries are actually the people who are closer to your heart than you would ever imagine. I have seen Roca forge relationships with partners that you would never imagine an agency like theirs would be able to do."
>
> VICTIM WITNESS ADVOCATE, DISTRICT ATTORNEY'S OFFICE

"I guess the word that I would use is trust. . . . I now
have trust that whatever they do, they do for the
right reasons, and it allows me to immediately defend
them to the city council, the D.A.s, or the police. The
D.A.'s office will call and say, 'That damn Roca was at
court, and this guy has a rap sheet a mile long, and
they're trying to defend him.' Well, I trust that they
are doing it for the right reasons."

CHELSEA CITY OFFICIAL

Doing the work of systemic change requires, therefore, "staying
in relationship" over the long haul, even when people don't agree.
Although Roca and these various institutions have different mis-
sions, agendas, ideas, cultures, and priorities, their positive relationships have created a reservoir of trust. This deep trust comes
from a shared sense of purpose.

Visioning Systemic Change

"One thing that Roca has shown the rest of us is that,
by working together, we can accomplish so much."

CHELSEA CITY OFFICIAL

Because the Circle is about creating a just community, the Circle
must also be a means for creating systemic change. It is no secret
that we currently live in societies that are profoundly imbalanced
and unjust. While the privileged may maintain a veil of denial
about social inequality, the painful truth of social injustice is
common knowledge among those who suffer from it everyday.

A sense of justice is a core element of what it means to be a human being. Justice matters to us as a species, and learning how to
live justly is critical to our moral development as individuals and as
a species. As Heraclitus observed, human beings learn what justice

is when we experience injustice. Schooled or not, people know when they are being treated unjustly. Holding a vision of justice is not, therefore, an idle fantasy or an abstract ideal. It is a practical strategy, because it focuses our intentions and shapes our behaviors. Guided by a vision of justice, we have some image of what we are trying to create. Yet, such a vision has value in the world only when it actually shapes how we behave in the world as well.

One of the great gifts that Roca has brought to its relationship with other institutions is that, as an organization, Roca models its vision of a just world where all young people are valued and belong. This steadfast vision has changed how the city manager sees gang members and "illegal immigrants" within his community. He no longer tries to figure out how to exclude them from the city. It has also changed how the Department of Youth Services thinks about its mission with young people: caseworkers consider the possibility that connecting with youth may be more valuable than controlling them. And it has affected school administrators' attitudes and policies toward "student misconduct." They now look for ways to partner with Roca and the community in order to keep even the "troublesome kids" engaged in school.

> "Roca has enlightened me to a whole group of people that I knew nothing about. Practically speaking, I've lived here all my life. That doesn't mean that I know what it's like to live here as a Latino or a street kid. What Roca has done is open up insight into that world and help me understand that not all gang members are bad. They are people. Some of them are looking for identity; some of them are looking for relationships that they lack back at home. There are any number of reasons why people join gangs. Now I am less concerned with bringing in Immigration and Naturalization services to get rid of all the illegal aliens, and I am more concerned about improving

the quality of life for anyone who lives here. I would
attribute all that to Roca."

CHELSEA CITY OFFICIAL

But visions can also increase a sense of powerlessness and contribute to paralysis, because they help us see the magnitude of
our problems. Unless visions are accompanied by a sense that our
actions can lead to a desired end, visions can leave us feeling overwhelmed. Those who work with youth know this feeling. Young
people who are out of school and out of work, gang-involved, carrying guns, engaged in prostitution, or dealing and using drugs
are merely symptoms of the world that adults create and re-create
every day.

When we treat young people as if they are the only part of
our world that needs to change, we fool ourselves with the belief
that it is the young people who are "the problem." Many adults
within our systems acknowledge that systemic change is needed,
but they remain paralyzed by a sense of helplessness. When a
principal expels a student, a parent signs a CHINS (Child in Need
of Services) petition, or a judge sentences an offender to prison,
that individual shifts the burden, hoping someone somewhere
else will solve the problem.

Ironically, those with the most social power—judges, commissioners, superintendents, and CEOs—often settle for solutions
that address only the most obvious symptoms, because that is
how they are trained. As a result, they end up feeling as powerless as everyone else about fundamental problems and how to
adequately address them. They may know that a young person
who carries a knife into school is not "the cause" of a widespread
social phenomenon that has schools across the country barricad-
ing their doors with metal detectors. They may also know that
their decision to expel a student will only increase the likelihood
that he or she will never graduate from high school and may also
end up in the adult correctional system. Yet even these powerful,

decision-making adults act as if they have no choice, because they see themselves as instruments of a system that dictates their actions. Those at the top of systems do not feel as if they possess the autonomy to make positive, creative, or courageous choices.

> "Many visions are doomed from the outset, because those who articulate them, whether consciously or not, are coming from a place of powerlessness. If we believe that someone else has created our present reality, what is the basis for believing that we can create a different reality in the future? When this happens, people formulate visions that are disconnected from a shared understanding of present reality and a sense of shared responsibility for that reality. If people are still externalizing their problems, they create, in a sense, 'externalized visions,' which amount to a kind of change strategy for fixing problems which they have not yet seen their part in creating. Only when people begin to see from within the forces that shape their reality and to see their part in how those forces might evolve does vision become powerful. Everything else is just a vague hope."
>
> SENGE ET AL.[3]

So while a vision is essential, it is equally important to embrace our ability to change the current reality. To do this, we must learn to look truthfully at the current situation and be willing to take responsibility for our own behavior in re-creating that reality. The truth of our situation is that many of our young people are neither valued nor cared for. Rather, they are treated with gross neglect, tossed aside, abused, exploited, excluded, and rejected by adults and the institutions we have created. This is a painful reality, and to begin to create a new reality, we need to learn how to have some hard conversations about our current failures.

"Parents, young people, community, and institutions,
even policy makers, politicians, law enforcement . . .
we are in relationship with them more than ever—
maybe more than we wished to be! It's still a lot of
work, but since we started using Circles, we can have
honest conversations, and that, to me, is a big shift
and a big change. We can have conversations about
education and be truthful and honest about it but in
a most gentle way, so we don't have to be yelling and
screaming. We can say, 'Look, whatever you are doing
is not working, and whatever we're doing is not working, so how do we work together to make it work?'

"So the relationships in the last two to three years
have been a kind of preparation phase to go to another
level of work in deepening the work we are trying to do
around healing. So more and more, we are in relationship in a most honest way. That's a big shift."

SAROEUM, ROCA STAFF

Although it is easy to forget, systems are made up of human beings. We both create and are created by our social systems. While
it is true that we are profoundly affected and shaped by the structures within which we live, it is also true that the very relationship we have with all the systems around us gives us the power
to change these systems and structures. Like all of life, systems
and structures are always changing. Because we are inescapably a
part of systems, we have the capacity to push back on them and
transform them. We may not be able to do this overnight, nor will
this happen through the autocratic command of any one person
or group in positions of power. But each of us can choose to be
responsible and to participate in creating significant long-term
change. The vision is one of stewardship rather than domination:
we take care of the future by continually taking our individual
actions each day.

Roca youth

As the wisdom of the blocks suggests, the choice to become aware, to be responsible for our own behavior, and to choose how we act toward others is the authentic source of power in the world. Hierarchical systems of oppression and control disempower us. Labels such as "offenders," "victims," "gang members," or "drug dealers"; social titles such as "doctor," "commissioner," or "judge"; and racial and gendered categories all impose filters through which we view one other. They shape what we assume to be true about each other and therefore directly affect how we treat one another.

But our spirits and psyches can challenge and reject these internal mechanisms of oppression and control. It is here in what we see, think, and value where we are truly in control. To use again the metaphor of Dorothy going home to Kansas, the power to bring justice home is here within us all along. Einstein said,

"Imagination is more important than knowledge." Restructuring our lives starts with unleashing our imaginations—becoming aware of how we can see, think, and feel and choosing to be with each other in different ways.

> "Circles can bring people together. . . . [They] can help them to understand each other, to heal on the inside, to accept themselves and their lives as they are, to walk in their ways. When I say to walk in their ways, I mean to accept reality, not to cover the world with powerlessness, to grab for a star that's out of reach; to walk in their ways means to have their identity and with that identity to struggle for themselves. I believe the Circle helps people to value themselves, to believe in themselves, and to know they are capable of accomplishing many things that they wish."
>
> SISTER JOSEFA, ROCA COMMUNITY PARTNER

Creating a Different Kind of Justice

> "I don't even like using the word 'justice,' because I think the justice we have now is defined as winning. . . . I think what people mean when they say 'justice' is they can say they won. The Circle? I don't know if you want to call it justice. I believe that it falls under the heading of healing and I don't think justice is winning. I think justice is healing."
>
> JAMES, ROCA STAFF

> "I think that the young people feel like there is not a lot of justice anywhere. They always say it too: 'At least you listen to us; the judge in the court never listens to us. He thinks justice is locking someone up.'"
>
> ANGIE, ROCA STAFF

Is the Circle a path toward justice? When asked about justice, young people at Roca are either confused or disgusted by the word. To them, "justice" is the business of the courts, police, and lock-ups. All of these reinforce a sense of domination and alienation that they experience in almost every sphere of their lives. The justice they know is adversarial and punitive: one side wins and another side loses. It leaves the underlying problems within the community unacknowledged, unaddressed, and unchanged. For them, justice is a cruel sideshow that does a lot of damage and has little relevance to the challenge of improving the grim realities of life within their communities. These young people are pretty clear that, whatever true justice may be, it has little to do with the state-administered system as it now operates. How can a system be just, they ask, that demonizes, blames, and punishes individuals, while failing to address the political, economic, and social inequalities of their lives, as if these systemic realities played no role in all that has happened?

> "If someone was abused as a child, their anger comes
> out. Does that give them the right to abuse their
> child? Maybe that person, too, was abused as a child.
> That doesn't make it right. But you see, these are
> the things that no one ever talks about. Maybe some
> people need to serve time, but I know people in jail
> right now. Being in jail is like being on the street.
> Same things, same issues, same people, same an-
> ger. . . . So where's your justice?"
>
> JAMES, ROCA STAFF

When asked if the Circle has anything to do with justice, however, these same young people express a very different understanding of justice. To them, the Circle feels like a place of authentic justice. Above all, it is a place of equality where each voice is heard. Justice is inseparable from a fundamental sense of equality and dignity. Being seen and heard are core elements of what it means to live in the world in a way that is just.

> "I think that Circles promote justice more than other places, because, first of all, fundamentally, it is a process of honoring people."
>
> ANISHA, ROCA STAFF

> "For me, justice means some sort of democracy, some sort of way of being without punishment—to me, that's justice. I wish the courts would do this, 'cause what they do is not justice. I think a lot has to do with just being able to talk to each other, . . . then a sort of justice is formed. For me, when we end a Circle, it feels like there was some sort of justice in here, because everybody got to talk, everybody got to say what they had to say."
>
> ANGIE, ROCA STAFF

> "The attraction of the Circle is justice. If you define justice as insuring every person's human right or giving every person their due because they are, then I think there's no better vehicle for demonstrating that than the Circle process, where every person is acknowledged, every person is valued. . . . Power is shared, and when that happens, it's magnified. That's justice."
>
> GREGG, TEACHER AND ROCA PARTNER

To the youth at Roca, justice is also a form of action that addresses the unmet needs of people within a community. Circles provide a vehicle for this action. Through Circles, community members express and thereby understand what is not working or even outright wrong in their life together. Circles also promote a sense that it is possible to marshal the community's collective resources to right these wrongs, to make things truly work for people, and to do whatever needs to be done in a good, community-based way.

As it is, communities suffer profound disempowerment. The very systems that have been created and funded to address their needs regularly exclude them. We come back to a core critique that restorative justice makes: our institutions consistently disempower the communities they are supposed to serve. Marshalling an array of professionals and experts, systems attempt to do the work "for" communities, instead of working *with* community members as full and equal partners.

Even with the best of intentions, this top-down approach is sure to fail. It cannot possibly satisfy needs as the community members themselves see them. The relationships between systems and communities are fraught with problems: conflicting agendas; emotions of anger and blame; time constraints; and patterns of miscommunication that reinforce barriers between people. On the system side, structures of power solidify as ingrained patterns of silence. On the community side, frustrations, rage at inequities and injustices, and resentments accumulate and eventually become overwhelming. Community members often feel that they cannot speak honestly about the painful issues within their communities, much less come to agreements about how to work toward solutions. They scarcely know where to begin.

> "Systems have made it so that you need special training to actually fix things, and I think that people buy into that all too much—the idea that people who have law degrees and everything else are the ones who can fix things."
>
> VICTIM ADVOCATE, DISTRICT ATTORNEY'S OFFICE

To create just communities, the Circle's first response and primary lesson is that we must include all members of the commu-

Roca youth and his son

nity to begin to work toward justice. Whether you are a systems person, citizen, immigrant, young person, ex-con, judge, teacher, gang member, or mayor, you are a part of the community, and your contribution is a necessary part of the solution. The Circle invites us to shift toward seeing ourselves and one another as equal participants who are accountable to each other. Through Circles, we begin to see one another beyond the assumptions and stereotypes that are a source of so much distrust and suspicion.

"We always feel strongly that we can fix other people's problems, and we believe in professionalism, but we never believe in ourselves. To me, the hopeful piece is that we don't have to fix anyone, but all we can do is help share our experience and our story, and the more we do that, the more we bring the will and human spirit among all of us collectively . . . that we have the ultimate gift."

SAROEUM, ROCA STAFF

The Circle creates a sense that it is possible to meet the needs of everyone and to redress the ongoing causes of harm and suffering. To the youth engaged in Circles, justice is about changing what is harmful and wrong in people's lives, so that they can heal from the past and live in the present with hope, security, and dignity. Justice is about actually changing the way we live together. It is about making sure that people are not harmed by the structural violence of institutions, so that, in turn, they do not cause harm to others. Justice is certainly about personal accountability, so that individuals take responsibility. But it is equally about political and social accountability among leaders, politicians, and the community, so that systemic injustices do not persist.

"Justice, I believe, is a way to finally find out what is going on with our society today—what is working and what is not working. And what is not working, we need to fix, and I believe that the Circle process can get to that. If we have to start here, we have to start here, because if we don't, we're gonna be doing the same things we're doing today thirty years from now. And the hope for that is that finally people can see all the hurt that they have caused—all the hurt that they have caused others—in the hope that people start holding themselves accountable and start finally saying, 'The way we live is not healthy. There's a better way, and we need to start figuring it out.'"

JAMES, ROCA STAFF

Young people at Roca are drawn to the Circle because it is an experience of being in relationships of respect, dignity, and compassion with other human beings. They sense that this is what justice is all about. This may not be what they have been taught "justice" means. Nonetheless, their own wisdom gives them a different understanding from the dominant view represented by our institutions of law and justice. In everyday life, justice is fundamentally a positive concept that has to do with living in a way that meets everyone's needs and that honors the dignity of all people.

> "Justice in the Circle with a shared vision and shared values may be a pure form of justice. The idea is that no one will get left behind, and everyone will feel good about this, and we all will have to come to the same conclusion. In the Circle process, there is no 'us and them'; it is 'we.' We made this mess, and we're gonna figure a way out. So it's a pure form of we—by action, by sharing, by moving together. No one will be left behind or feel like they are not being heard or respected. I think it means that everybody's needs are met. To me, that is justice."

SAROEUM, ROCA STAFF

To Roca's young people, the Circle is a place where genuine healing takes place. Yet this involves far more than healing individuals alone. Young people intuitively sense that the Circle holds the promise for social change. By coming together to be in a different kind of relationship with one another, young people gain hope that we might together find a way to address the destructive cycles of pain and suffering that churn through our lives. From their experiences in Circles, they gain a profound hopefulness that brilliantly ordinary people can come together in a good way and, by so doing, discover the extraordinary will to create a way of living together that is just.

Notes

Chapter Two: Urban Youth and Modern Monsters

1. Sources for data about Chelsea and Roca youth include: U.S. Census Bureau: State and County Quick Facts; data derived from Population Estimates, 2000 Census of Population and Housing; Massachusetts Department of Education (DOE): 2002 Selected Populations Report (District), Boston, MA: DOE *http://profiles.doe.mass.edu*; Massachusetts Department of Public Health, Bureau of Health Statistics, Research and Evaluation, 2000; Chelsea Public Schools Youth Risk Behavior Survey, 2000; Massachusetts Department of Public Health, Bureau of Health Statistics, Research and Evaluation, 2000; Massachusetts Department of Health, Adolescent Births: A Statistical Profile, 2000.

2. Robert Yazzie, "Life Comes from It: Navajo Justice Concepts," *New Mexico Law Review* 24 (Spring 1994): 176–77.

3. Chelsea Public Schools Youth Risk Behavior Survey, 2003.

4. Christopher Uggen and Sara Wakefield, "Young Adults Reentering the Community from the Criminal Justice System: The Challenge of Becoming an Adult," in *On Your Own Without a Net: The Transition to Adulthood for Vulnerable Populations,* ed. D. Wayne Osgood, E. Michael Foster, Constance Flanagan, and Gretchen R. Ruth (Chicago: University of Chicago Press, 2005).

5. Mark E. Courtney and Darcy Hughes Heuring, "The Transition to Adulthood for Youth 'Aging Out' of the Foster Care System," in *On Your Own Without a Net,* ed. Osgood, et al.

6. Massachusetts Department of Health, *Adolescent Births: A Statistical Profile, 2000;* Anne E. Casey Foundation, *Moving Youth from Risk to Opportunity,* www.aecf.org/kidscount (2003).

7. W. H. Sack, G. N. Clarke, and John Seeley, "Posttraumatic Stress Disorder Across Two Generations of Cambodian Refugees," *Journal of American Academy of Child and Adolescent Psychiatry* 34, no. 9 (1995): 1160–67.

8. Ana Arana, "How Street Gangs Took Central America," *Foreign Affairs* (May/June, 2005).

9. Peter Senge, C. Otto Scharmer, Joseph Jaworski, and Betty Sue Flowers, *Presence: An Exploration of Profound Change in People, Organizations and Society* (New York: Random House, 2003), 4.

10. Larry K. Brendtro, Rev. Dr. Martin Brokenleg, and Steve Van Bockern, *Reclaiming Youth At Risk: Our Hope for the Future* (Bloomington, IN: National Educational Service, 1990), revised edition with foreword by Archbishop Desmond Tutu (Bloomington, IN: Solution Tree, 2002).

11. Kay Pranis, Barry Stuart, and Mark Wedge, *Peacemaking Circles: From Crime to Community* (Saint Paul, MN: Living Justice Press, 2003).

Chapter Three: The Circle as a Strategy in Youth Development

1. As quoted in S. Beth Atkins, *Voices from the Streets: Young Former Gang Members Tell Their Stories* (New York: Little Brown & Co., 1996), 23.

2. Ibid., 24.

3. Ibid., 26.

4. Jean E. Rhodes, *Stand By Me: The Risks and Rewards of Mentoring Today's Youth* (Cambridge, MA: Harvard University Press, 2002).

5. John Braithwaite, "Youth Development Circles," *Oxford Review of Education* 27 (2001): 239–52.

6. Bethany Casarjian and Robin Casarjian, *Power Source: Taking Charge of Your Life* (Boston: Lionheart Foundation, 2003).

7. Kenneth Polk, "Positive Youth Development, Restorative Justice and the Crisis of Abandoned Youth," in *Restorative Community Justice: Repairing Harm and Transforming Communities,* ed. Gordon Bazemore and Mara Schiff (Cincinnati, OH: Anderson, 2001).

8. D. Wayne Osgood, E. Michael Foster, Constance Flanagan, and Gretchen R. Ruth, eds., *On Your Own Without a Net: The Transition to Adulthood for Vulnerable Populations* (Chicago: University of Chicago Press, 2005).

Chapter Four: The Circle as a Space of Empowerment

1. Robert Yazzie, "Life Comes From It: Navajo Justice Concepts," *New Mexico Law Review*, 24 (Spring 1994): 188.

2. Kaethe Weingarten, "Witnessing, Wonder and Hope," *Family Process* 30, no. 4 (2000): 390–412.

Chapter Five: The Circle as a Space of Accountability

1. John Braithwaite and D. Roche, "Responsibility and Restorative Justice," in *Restorative Community Justice: Repairing Harm and Transforming Communities,* ed. Gordon Bazemore and Mara Schiff (Cincinnati, OH: Anderson, 2001).

2. John Braithwaite, "Youth Development Circles," *Oxford Review of Education* 27 (2001): 239–52.

Chapter Six: The Circle as a Space for Healing

1. Judith Lewis Herman, *Trauma and Recovery* (New York: Basic Books, 1992), 51–52.

2. Ibid., 133.

3. Ibid., 55.

4. James Gilligan, *Violence: Reflections on a National Epidemic* (New York: Random House, 1996), 188.

5. Ibid., 48.

6. Kaethe Weingarten, *Common Shock: Witnessing Violence Everyday: How We Are Harmed and How We Can Heal* (New York: Penguin, 2003).

7. Herman, *Trauma and Recovery,* 53.

8. As quoted in S. Beth Atkins, *Voices from the Streets: Young Former Gang Members Tell Their Stories* (New York: Little Brown & Co., 1996), 20.

9. Archbishop Desmond Tutu, *No Future without Forgiveness* (London: Rider, 1999).

10. Robin Casarjian, *Houses of Healing: A Prisoner's Guide to Inner Power and Freedom* (Boston: Lionheart Foundation, 1998).

11. Bethany Casarjian and Robin Casarjian, *Power Source: Taking Charge of Your Life* (Boston: Lionheart Foundation, 2003).

12. Weingarten, *Common Shock,* 218.

13. Ibid., 219.

14. Herman, *Trauma and Recovery,* 214.

Chapter Seven: Opening the Heart within Systems

1. Barry D. Stuart, *R. v. Jacob,* 2002 YKTC 15 Territorial Court of the Yukon Territory, Whitehorse, Canada (2002): 20.

2. John McKnight, *The Careless Society: Community and Its Counterfeits* (New York: Basic Books, 1995).

3. Peter Senge, Art Kleiner, Charlotte Roberts, Richard Ross, George Roth, and Bryan Smith, *The Dance of Change: The Challenges to Sustaining Momentum in Learning Organizations* (New York: Doubleday, 1999), 49.

Chapter Eight: Bringing Justice Home

1. Peter Senge, C. Otto Scharmer, Joseph Jaworski, and Betty Sue Flowers, *Presence: An Exploration of Profound Change in People, Organizations and Society* (New York: Random House, 2003), 45–47.

2. Ibid., 193.

3. Ibid., 132.

Selected Bibliography

Atkin, S. Beth. *Voices from the Streets: Young Former Gang Members Tell Their Stories*. New York: Little Brown & Co., 1996.

Brendtro, Larry K., Martin Brokenleg, and Steve Van Bockern. *Reclaiming Youth At Risk: Our Hope for the Future*. Bloomington, IN: National Educational Service, 1990. Revised edition with foreword by Archbishop Desmond Tutu. Bloomington, IN: Solution Tree, 2002.

Casarjian, Robin. *Houses of Healing: A Prisoner's Guide to Inner Power and Freedom*. Boston: Lionheart Press, 1995.

Casarjian, Robin, and Bethany Casarjian. *Power Source: Taking Charge of Your Life*. Boston: Lionheart Press, 2003.

Gilligan, James. *Violence: Reflections on a National Epidemic*. New York: Vintage Books, 1996.

Herman, Judith. *Trauma and Recovery: The Aftermath of Violence—From Domestic Abuse to Political Terror*. New York: Basic Books, 1992, 1997.

Pranis, Kay, Barry Stuart, and Mark Wedge. *Peacemaking Circles: From Crime to Community*. Saint Paul, MN: Living Justice Press, 2003.

Senge, Peter. *The Fifth Discipline: The Art and Practice of the Learning Organization*. New York: Doubleday Currency, 1990.

Senge, Peter, Art Kleiner, Charlotte Roberts, Richard Ross, George Roth, and Bryan Smith. *The Dance of Change: The Challenges to Sustaining Momentum in Learning Organizations*. New York: Currency, 1999.

Senge, Peter, C. Otto Scharmer, Joseph Jaworski, and Betty Sue Flowers. *Presence: An Exploration of Profound Change in People, Organizations and Society*. New York: Random House, 2004.

Stuart, Barry. *R v. Jacob, 2002 Yukon Territorial Court 15*. Territorial Court of the Yukon Territory, Whitehorse, Canada.

Weingarten, Kaethe. *Common Shock: Witnessing Violence Every Day: How We Are Harmed and How We Can Heal*. New York: Dutton, 2003.

Yazzie, Robert. "Life Comes from It: Navajo Justice Concepts." *New Mexico Law Review*, 24 (Spring 1994).

Index

"abandoned youth," 29, 43, 54, 71–72, 232n. 7
Aboriginal traditions, 12, 58
abuse, 5, 139: of children, 23, 144, 224; consequences of, 158; sexual, 50, 170; and silence, 156; substance, 19, 51, 67–68, 105, 129, 178, 250; and success in mentoring, 50; and trauma, 143–44; and violence, 145; youth's experience of, 220
accountability, 109–113, 129, 133–36, 163: and Circle process, 31, 61, 85, 109, 112–13, 118, 120, 127, 227; and competence, 110; and guidelines, 118, 120; and healing, 138, 163–64, 167; how Circles promote, 123, 127; and independence, 110; as learned through relationships, 112; and maturing to adulthood, 111–12; and modeling, 54, 129–31; as mutual, 61, 85, 103, 109, 136, 227; as part of adulthood, 111; practicing, 6, 110; as principle of justice, 6, 136, 228–29; and punishment, 111, 113, 118, 132, 138; Roca's to youth, 33, 35; in transformational relationships, 46, 48, 53
accountable, and holding oneself, 110, 113, 120, 133–36, 138
acknowledging: another's presence, 91–92; consequences and harm,

111, 133, 138, 146, 161; each other's wholeness, 136; and empathy, 161, 163; grief, 165–67; and healing, 150, 163–64
adolescence: as time for individuation, 103–104; and transition to adulthood, 25, 67–69, 124–25
adulthood: passage to, 23–25, 30, 67–69, 71, 91, 110; requirements for, 110–11; and taking responsibility, 111
adults, 10, 114: as coercive and manipulative of youth, 92, 99–100, 114–15; and developing individuality, 103–104; hypocrisy of, 130; and modeling for youth, 54; must change too, 76, 219; as not hearing youth, 92–93; and power imbalance with youth, 142; power and privilege of, 96–98; as promoting accountability in youth, 110–12; and relationships with youth, 30, 43, 49–52, 74; role of, in Circles with youth, 112–13; role of, in youth development, 15–16, 23, 30, 47, 49–52, 54, 70, 105, 124–25, 159; and sharing stories with youth, 112–13, 123, 130–31, 170; youth's mistrust of, 117–18, 143. See also adolescence, adulthood, mentoring, transformational relationships

76; through creativity and vision,
184–85; and feelings, 150; as
free choice, 200, 202; gateways
to, 203–204; as incremental, 76,
86, 112; from individual action,
221; as involving both youth and
adults, 75–76, 219; toward justice,
217, 228; and leading, 17, 35, 38,
43, 199–203; modeling, 202; need
for, 182–84; as nonlinear, 76; and
offenders, 138, 162; in organizations, 34, 184–89, 199–204; as
painful, 199; from people, 201; as
problem-solving, 184; relationships promote, 45, 48–49, 53, 55,
66, 74, 77; resistance to, 199–200;
and restorative justice, 8; as Roca's
goal for youth, 48–49, 74–77;
in Roca's organization, 11, 40,
185–88, 212–14; of rules, 114, 116;
and setbacks, 52, 74, 76; in social
institutions, 34, 75–77; systemic,
7, 34, 71–73, 75–76, 182–84,
217–22; as uncomfortable, 49, 77;
as value-based, 34, 39–40, 201;
youth leading, 35, 38, 43, 49, 67.
See also transformation, transformational relationships

Chelsea (Massachusetts): demographics of, 19–23, 231n. 1; and Department of Social Services, 181, 183;
economic statistics for, 18; and
gangs, 28–29; immigrant peoples
of, 20–21, 27, 60; and quotes from
city officials, 19–20, 213, 217–19;
Roca's location in, 16–17; statistics
about youth in, 24, 26

Child in Need of Services (CHINS),
71, 219

Circles: as about us, 86, 201–203; and
accountability, 6, 85, 109–113,
123, 129–30, 136; and agreeing
on guidelines, 85, 88–89, 114–16,

118–22; as balancing commonalities and differences, 104–105,
206; basics of, 59; and belonging,
66, 91, 103–104; and blocks exercise, 207–211; as bringing out our
"best selves," 3; as bringing out
our talents, wisdom, energies, 6,
79, 104–108; as building networks
of support, 62–64, 127–28; as
building relationships, 3, 5, 61, 74;
champions of, in organizations,
175–82; for collective visioning,
74; and community building, 6,
215–17; and community collaboration, 73, 212–15; and compassionate witnessing, 6, 150; for conflict
resolution, 61–62; for creating
consensus, 88; as creating mutual
understanding, 192–94; as democratic process, 58, 114–16; and
developing empathy, 161–62; as
distinct process, 9–10; egalitarian
structure of, 58, 81–82; and emotional awareness, 6; and gangs,
61; and generosity of sharing our
gifts, 104–108; as a gift, 11–14, 83;
as giving voice to those marginalized, 6, 100–103, 189; and healing,
6, 64, 139–41, 146–48, 150, 171;
for healing, 64; hidden lessons of,
83–86, 210–11; and "holding the
space," 89, 100, 103; Indigenous
origins of, 3; and invitation to,
99–100; and justice, 3–9, 131–38,
205, 207, 223–30; and keepers,
89; for leading change, 199–203;
and learning how to "be in a good
way," 8–9; and Medicine Wheel,
82–83; mentors of, to Roca,
11–12; and modeling responsibility, 6; and moving toward
balance, 82; openings and closings
of, 87–88; for organizational

Author Information

Carolyn Boyes-Watson is the founding director of Suffolk University's Center for Restorative Justice and an associate professor of sociology at Suffolk University. Professor Boyes-Watson has been on the faculty since 1993. She holds a bachelor's degree from the University of Pennsylvania and a master's and Ph.D. in sociology from Harvard University. She lives in Cambridge, Massachusetts, with her husband, Mark, and her two children, Emily and Matthew.

Contact information:
Department of Sociology
Suffolk University
8 Ashburton Place
Boston, Massachusetts 02108
Phone: (617) 573-8085
Fax: (617) 994-4278
E-mail: cwatson@suffolk.edu

Further Comments from
the Community about Circles and Youth

Publishers regularly seek comments about the books they publish to encourage potential readers to buy the books and read them. We at Living Justice Press are most grateful for the comments submitted to us by a number of restorative justice professionals and community members who have taken the time to read the manuscript and share their thoughts about it. Some of these comments appear at the front of this book and others here.

In addition to commenting about *Peacemaking Circles and Urban Youth*, we also invited these pre-publication readers to share some of their experiences of using Circles with youth. Roca's work is clearly extraordinary, yet Roca is by no means alone in using Circles with youth. Many people—teachers, principals, administrators, juvenile justice staff, lawyers, judges, and youth workers—are using Circles with young people in all sorts of contexts and are having similarly powerful and transformative experiences. We want to support the power of Roca's work with proof that Circles are profoundly changing both youth and the adults who share their lives not only in Chelsea but across the country as well.

For anyone who seeks to appreciate the difference between restorative justice as a technique and as a way of life, this is a "must read" book. Carolyn Boyes-Watson has captured how lives and organizations change when the values, principles, and processes of peacemaking Circles are immersed into our personal lives and into the larger communities of the workplace and neighborhoods we share. After ROCA's initial introduction to Circles years ago, I asked Molly Baldwin when she might start using Circles. She answered, "Not until I have 200 people trained. I see Circles not as something we might do but as the way we live."

Roca engages Circles not as a technique to use when conflict happens but when life happens. In this way, the ideals of peacemaking Circles are carried to their full potential to reinforce a way of being and to serve as a foundation for all interactions, whether the interactions are rooted in joy or in pain.

This book reveals the pioneering trail blazed by ROCA—a trail that others as individuals or groups will want to travel. The experience of ROCA will inspire others to develop their own way to an environment that calls out the best parts of our ability to connect to others. There are insights in the telling of ROCA's story to be developed by individuals, schools, corporations, government departments, or communities. In fact, it can inspire anyone who seeks ways to build environments that use differences and conflicts as opportunities to generate innovative outcomes and effective working relationships. Circles create environments where personal values are not parked outside but become the foundation for interactions.

This is a history that will change the future. . . . Thank you, ROCA, for marking out the potential of relationships to others based on the principles and processes of peacemaking Circles and value-based restorative justice practices.

—Barry D. Stuart

Chief Judge, Yukon (retired); Coauthor of Peacemaking Circles: From Crime to Community; *Principal Partner, CSE Consulting Group Associate, Morris J. Wosk Centre for Dialogue, Adjunct Professor, Criminology, Simon Fraser University, Vancouver, British Columbia, Canada*

Respect, humility, compassion, spirituality, and honesty: where do we talk about these values? We discuss them in our Washington County Community Circles, because they are the foundation for our work in Sentencing Circles. Just like Roca, we try to create a respectful space for participants to be listened to and treated as equals. When this happens, we have seen youth share moving, insightful, and powerful thoughts, ideas, and experiences.

Life is a journey of change. There are times in all of our lives when we need to change. Circles provide a process for community members to share their journeys with participants in the process. As community members, we have the privilege of sharing in the transformation that only the participants themselves can make. The sooner in our lives any of us can make these changes, the better our lives will be.

The Minnesota and Roca Circle communities are fortunate to have been trained in the same value-based Circle way by our friends and mentors from the Yukon Territory. Our family feels that the spirituality of the Circle process connects us to the Roca community. We are inspired by the stories from Roca, and humbly thank them for their dedication to our mutual values.

—Gary, Lynn, and Katie Schurrer

Gary is a District Court Judge and has been a Circle Council Member in Washington County Community Circles in Minnesota since 1997. Gary's wife Lynn and their daughter Katie are Circle Keepers and have participated in Washington County Community Circles since 1999.

As I write on the fortieth anniversary of the assassination of The Reverend Dr. Martin Luther King, I reflect on how saddened he would be to see the disparate numbers of people of color now incarcerated in United States prisons. Of the 2.38 million people currently incarcerated in federal and state prisons and jails, African Americans alone make up 38 percent: 905,000 people. In several states, the incarceration rates of African Americans are more than ten times the rates that Whites are incarcerated.

On the other hand, I believe that Dr. King would be encouraged by the rise of restorative justice programs such as Roca, which is profiled in *Peacemaking Circles and Urban Youth*. As I read about Roca, I thought about my own experiences with the Circle process and our efforts to reclaim people who would otherwise have become part of these statistics. One of the reasons that Circles are so effective is that they provide an alternative means by which people can avoid being processed by an impersonal criminal justice system. In Roca's story, I saw people facing the same problems that we faced with clients, community members, and people from the justice system. I was reminded that it is not only not unusual but also probable that there will be mistrust between the clients and those from the criminal justice system, partly because this is merely the expression of longstanding animosities, and also because the Circle process, though based on ancient traditions, is so new and untested in modern society. However, when a core group of committed people stay with the process, most of those who are distrusting eventually come around and see how beneficial the Circle process can be.

The work that is being done at Roca is in the best traditions of Circles, because it gives youth an opportunity to pursue positive life goals. We can only hope that Roca's example will spread across the country, and other communities will begin to experience the magic of the Circle process, so that they, too, can stem the flow of youth to jails and prisons.

—Judge Edward Wilson
State District Court Judge in St. Paul, Minnesota

Peacemaking Circles and Urban Youth illustrates the power of Circles in a unique environment. It tells the story of a youth development program, known as Roca, that serves "high risk" young people in one of the most densely populated, impoverished, ethnically diverse, and troubled communities in the United States. Roca uses Circles as an essential, democratic, decision-making process as well as a respectful and powerful way of communicating. At Roca, Circles are a way of "being," grounded in a restorative justice and youth development philosophy and practice. They are aimed ultimately at building new communities [in the sense of MLK's "Beloved Community"] both inside the Roca community and in Chelsea neighborhoods. *Peacemaking Circles and Urban Youth* suggests how Circles could transform communities—broadly including schools, neighborhoods, residential facilities, and, as Boyes-Watson shows, even the social services systems charged with assisting them.

—Gordon Bazemore
> *Author of* Juvenile Justice Reform and Restorative Justice *and* Restorative Juvenile Justice *and Chair of the Department of Criminology and Criminal Justice at Florida Atlantic University*

Carolyn Boyes-Watson has brought to life the wonderful, empowering work of Roca. This book provides the reader with an easy-to-grasp understanding of the humanizing power of the restorative process of Circles. Anyone concerned with the state of our young people—and especially justice and school officials—cannot help but be transformed by these stories. In fact, it is likely that many people's thinking about the term "justice" will be challenged—and transformed.

—David Lerman
> *Restorative Justice Prosecutor for Milwaukee's public schools and Director of the Community Conferencing Program for the Milwaukee County District Attorney's Office*

It is so important for us to record our history, our stories. For many years, Roca has had an incredibly generous spirit of sharing their time, materials, resources, experiences, knowledge, and stories, from which so many of us have benefited. They are among the forerunners of applying the ancient Indigenous wisdom to the urban communities.

Thank you, Roca, for telling your story. May the wisdom of its lessons continue to be our northern star.

—Ora Schub
Circle Keeper and Trainer for the Community Justice for Youth Institute in Chicago

I am not sure if I can capture in words how inspired I was while reading this book. It is truly a gem! It captures the true spirit of Circle and the space Circle allows for that unconditional love that was meant to be shared. This book will be a great asset for those of us who advocate for the use of restorative justice while providing opportunities for our youth. Please give my thanks to all who were involved in this initiative. Wow!

—Jeanette Martinez
Jeanette is the Division Director of Outcomes Inc., a nonprofit agency that promotes restorative justice in New Mexico. The agency works in collaboration with Juvenile Probation and Parole in providing restorative justice Circles to young offenders who committed a violent crime or who are incarcerated. Judges and district attorneys regularly refer cases to Jeanette's organization for them to hold healing Circles, reintegration Circles, homicide Circles, and conflict Circles.

From an urban educator's perspective, *Peacemaking Circles and Urban Youth* reminded me that, with the right organizational structures and an open heart, teachers and students can resolve conflict and learn together. The young voices woven throughout the text are proof that punitive systems perpetuate alienation and hopelessness in our youth. Peacemaking Circles provide a structure to help us listen, understand, not condemn, and not push away young people when they make mistakes. Roca is an example of the kind of accountability system that works—one with persistence, support, compassion, and a deep honor for community as the agent of social justice.

> **—Adina Schecter**
> *Teacher at an urban public school, who uses Circles in her inner city high school classroom*

Another Circle team member and myself were invited to share the Circle process with students at a junior high school—about 300 students in all. In their literature class, they had been reading a novel where a restorative justice Circle was used. The staff and students wanted to know about actual Circles and if their impact was similar to what the main character in the novel had experienced. We explained the Circle process to them and used metaphors, like a puzzle, to help the students connect with how pieces of one's life can be restored.

The teachers were amazed at how interested the students were in learning about the Circle process and experiencing it, especially students who, at times, found it difficult to pay attention for long periods. The students embraced the process, which helped them to create a safe place for their voices to be heard. We shared with the youth our understanding of respect and discussed with them the values they wished to hold for this Circle. They chose overwhelmingly honesty, respect, and trust. Having this discussion on values helped curtail actions that the teachers had mentioned might be difficult during the Circle.

We used metaphors to make the discussion of these values concrete: What happens to a feather if you stroke it the wrong way? Doing this to a feather leaves the feather altered in appearance;

it is an inappropriate way to treat a feather. How does disrespect make you feel? What does respect feel like? Storytelling is another excellent tool to prompt youth to think more deeply and to open up. I'll read or tell a story and pass the talking piece, posing questions to help them focus. It's amazing how they respond and some even express the whole process as spiritual or sacred.

The teachers acknowledged that skills were needed in order to facilitate Circles. They witnessed youth participating openly and shared how they saw the Circle as a process for youth to express what they have on their minds about relationships in their school, their community, and in their families.

For years, I have held Circles for youth in trouble with the law. The Circle gives them an opportunity to face everyone: victims, parents, classmates and community people. When facilitating Circles for youth, I have found it helpful to have a man and a woman keep the Circle, so the youth see a balance in sharing that they may not experience at home. Ten years ago, a few of us developed a Circle at the Dakota County Juvenile Detention Center for young people facing more serious crimes. The Circle continues to be important to the youth there. Probation officers, police, and judges, at times, sit in Circle. In peacemaking Circles and Circles of support or understanding, I have found that youth are given an opportunity to experience the broader human impact of their actions and, through consensus, to reach ways of making restitution and making healing happen.

In order to facilitate Circles, Circle keepers, like myself, receive training and certification. This training has been provided by Native American elders and continues to be taught by them and others in our universities, like the University of Minnesota and Hamline University.

—Patricia Thalhuber, B.V.M.

Coauthor of Building a Home for the Heart: Using Metaphors in Value-Centered Circles; Community Developer who uses Circles as a process for healing

❁

Anytime we dispel ignorance and fear and allow people to have a voice, we improve our community tenfold. It is more difficult to do crimes against those you are in relationship with. The key is the relationships.

—Mark LaPointe,
Keeya Louta Mahto (Red Turtle Bear)

Along with his wife, Kay Longtin, Mark LaPointe, Canadian Cree Metis, has served as Circle Keeper and Trainer for youth and adults since 1999. They live in Cottage Grove, Minnesota.

We have been doing some Circle work with kids, though a lot of our work is with adults now. Not too long ago, Mary Sheppard, an advocate for the Tubman/Chrysalis Family Alliance, did a Circle for a group of twenty-four high school girls. All the girls had some form of violence in their lives—domestic abuse, violence from their boyfriends, school and street violence, bullying, drug violence. One young girl who is fifteen said that so many people were going in and out of her house because of her mother's and grandmother's addictions that she had to be the adult, the one who took responsibility. We're finding that with more and more young people. They need a place to talk. Circles give them that place where they can be safe, and everyone has a chance to participate equally.

We did a Circle with youth in New Jersey about race. Growing up in a multicultural community, they had no problem with each other. It's only when they get with adults that race issues come up. Adults need to be more aware, more sensitive in how they act. We can't say, "Don't do that" and then go out and do it ourselves. Young people notice that. We talk about "diversity and race" but then we talk badly about people. That's not good.

Circles allow us to have these discussions and to hold ourselves accountable. That's because Circles make it possible for us to do that in a good way. Circles give everyone a chance to talk. They create a safety net. Because everyone can be part of it, the discussion doesn't get one-sided. No one gets to dominate.

But it can take time for young people to get comfortable enough to talk, even in a Circle. At that Circle we did in New Jersey, one young man, an Asian American youth, kept passing the talking piece, and that's okay. Then, when we were almost done, he talked, and he had a lot to say! He had to decide if he could trust everyone, because the Circle was made up of everyone he knew. But they were opening up and sharing, so he finally got to the point where he felt he could as well.

Today, things are so different, even from three to four years ago. I think the Internet has a lot to do with that. Blogs go up about hating someone. There's bullying over the Internet. Parents are younger and more of them are on drugs, and their parents are on drugs too. Young people are dealing with a lot of intergenerational drug use. Gangs are replacing family, because so many youth have lost their family or run away. When I was growing up, the big thing for teenage girls was the fear of getting pregnant. Now it's prostitution, HIV, drug abuse. More than ever, youth need a safe place to talk through all that they're facing and get support. They need to create a community that will help them get on a good path. Unlike anywhere else in their lives, Circles provide a place where they can do this.

—Alice O. Lynch

Circle Trainer and Facilitator based in North Minneapolis, Circle of Parents Metro Coordinator, Talking Circle Coordinator for The Science Museum of Minnesota's RACE Exhibit, and former Executive Director of BIHA [Black, Indian, Hispanic, and Asian Women in Action]

Adults are absent; poverty, class and race barriers abound; our systems are stressed; youth gangs serve as surrogate parents; violence and disorder become the norm. Clearly, something needs to change. While we ask, "How can youth change?" we should be asking, "How can we change?" How can our youth-service delivery systems change?

This book shows us how Roca provides the desperately needed, consistent, caring, non-violent relationships that all youth must have for their healthy development. Roca has worked hard to establish a model organization that, with the use of peacemaking Circles, is able to continue to adapt in order to effectively serve its youth. Peacemaking Circles are the essential strategy in this journey of change, helping youth to turn their lives around against great odds and building caring communities along the way.

—Eva E. Marszewski
*Founder and Executive Director, Peacebuilders International
(Canada)*

◈

I have been working with youth for nine or ten years as an outreach worker. I have worked throughout the city of Chicago in a number of communities, including Englewood, Marquette, McKinley Park, Bridgeport, Back of the Yards, Brighton Park, Little Village, Pilsen, North Lawndale, South Lawndale, Humboldt Park, Logan Square, Belmont Cragin, Hermosa, and Westtown. I have also done outreach work in the Chicago Projects, including Stateway Gardens, Cabrini-Green, Robert Taylor Homes, ABLA, Lathrop Homes, and Rockwell Gardens.

The Circle training I attended has helped me be at peace with myself and receive healing in my life. It has made an impact on me and changed me. Through the training and by doing Circles, I have made a personal paradigm shift. I believe that you really have to experience for yourself this kind of change from Circles to really be able to do Circles effectively with youth. They can see right through you, and they know if something is not real, not genuine. Circles really do have to be a way of being, a way of life. Circles change you in your mind.

Youth always want and need a place where they can be heard, a place where they can have a voice. They need to express their feelings. They also want to talk about the hard, ugly, painful things in their lives. Circles provide that space. It is a safe space for them to be free and to express their feelings. At first, they don't want to do Circles. They don't know what it is. But once they learn how Circles work—the process—they get into it and ask questions. Once they experience it, they are more open to it.

I recently had a good experience with two young ladies, who started to open up in Circle. One of them talked about her father's heroin addiction and how painful it was for her to live with her father. She was expressing these painful feelings to the whole group. Well, as the talking piece went around, everyone gave her support and advice. Then, because the first lady opened up, the second one did too. She talked about her parents' alcoholism. Everyone embraced the hurt and pain of what these two young women were going through, and the Circle created the space for them to do that. Maybe some youth don't buy into the Circle right away, but even if they just sit there and listen, you can see it working on them.

It's the personal experiences that get them. If they see that Circles have helped you or someone else, they become more open. It feels genuine. You have to let that experience be real and heal you first, so that it becomes a way of being. Circles become a part of you. The Circle way stays at the forefront of your thinking. It becomes natural, automatic.

Not too long ago, a young man was shot. He had just started coming to the Circles. His death was gang-related. So, we held a Circle. They talked about grieving, but other problems in their lives came up too. One person was upset at being expelled; another was struggling with being homeless; someone else had just lost a parent. Because so many issues came up, we had a second Circle to focus on this young man's death. The young people were very direct: "He took his own life in his hands by choosing that lifestyle." "My boys were killed because of him." They grieved too, but they spoke very honestly.

From there, the youth raised other issues that needed to come up about the school. They felt frustrated. So I put it to them: "How can we make the changes we need to make here?" "How can we deal with the issues we have, such as attendance?" "How can we help each other deal with the family issues that come up?" Using Circles is helping to create a school family, and the youth are taking responsibility for the school. The Circle puts the ball in their court. They're taking responsibility for making the school a more restorative justice place—more about working together, less about punishment. Circles provide a space where youth can bring solutions to the problems we have in the school.

Because more Circle trainings are being offered all over the city, people from all walks of life are learning about Circles and using them. More and more agencies in the communities are going to trainings and buying into the process. Probation officers have been very keen to learn about Circles and use them with youth. Churches, schools, law enforcement, counselors: they're all experiencing what Circles can do for young people. It's a movement that is going on throughout the city.

But you have to start with yourself. You have to know yourself first. That's key. You have to know your weaknesses, how you got here, who you are. If you don't do that, you're not going to be effective or have an impact on the youth. Spiritually, mentally, in every way, you have to let the Circle bring you along.

For so many years, I have been working with youth who are at high risk. I would ask myself, "How can I be of better help to these young people? How can I help them deal with so many things that are going on in their lives?" Circles answer that.

—Sixto Torres
*Outreach Worker, Community Liaison, Counselor, Rudy Lozano
Leadership Academy, Pilsen Little Village, Chicago*

The Precious Blood Ministry of Reconciliation (PBMR) is a community-based project that strives to promote and practice restorative justice. We are located in the Back-of-the-Yards community on the southwest side of Chicago. Our community is comprised of African American and Hispanic families. A viaduct separates the communities, and we are located purposely at that boundary/border. Over the years, we have become deeply committed to the peacemaking Circle process, because it enables us to come together and be our best selves.

In our own Back-of-the-Yards community, we invite youth who are released from Cook County Juvenile Temporary Detention Center (especially those released from the southwest side of Chicago) to participate in weekly peacemaking Circles that we hold here at the Center (5114 S. Elizabeth St.). Beyond the regular peacemaking Circles, we also work to help the youth successfully re-enter into the community.

PBMR holds monthly healing Circles for families who have lost a loved one to violence. These Circles are in English and Spanish. Recently, we have included a Circle for teens to help them share their pain and anger at losing a sibling or close friend.

PBMR has conducted Circle in-services in a number of school and community groups. We have outreached into the religious communities by offering peacemaking training in the form of retreats. And we have hosted a number of Circle trainings here at the Center in collaboration with other groups. We are committed to collaborating with the members of our community.

Reflecting on our work with youth in an urban environment, for the past six or seven years, the Precious Blood Ministry of Reconciliation has used peacemaking Circles as a means of gathering and creating a safe place for youth who are detained or recently detained in the Cook County Juvenile Temporary Detention Center and/or the Illinois Department of Corrections. Inside the Cook County Juvenile Temporary Detention Center, we presently have three ongoing Circle programs:

a. a drumming and peacemaking Circle for boys being
   held on adult petitions;
b. a peacemaking Circle for boys on juvenile petitions; and
c. a peacemaking Circle for girls being held on juvenile
   petitions and adult petitions.

Every other Friday, we hold a drumming circle in Cook County Juvenile Detention Center. Fifteen to seventeen youths gather, each with a drum behind their chair. We use African djembe drums and a scattering of other percussion instruments. Drumming on djembes is a form of communication. We don't always know what message we are sending. We are simply attempting to call out that we are all caught up in life's rhythms and that we find our own sometimes thrashing cadence through it all.

These varied rhythms of the drums sound out, so that even the staff down the hall sometimes get caught up in the rhythm. There is something good about having a chance to build a sense of harmony and rhythm in what can be a hard place for young people—or anyone—to be. Occasionally, we experience quality moments when the overriding beat of the hefty junjun carries our flailing hands into a unified sound. Much of the time, though, it's just a circle of individuals releasing tension, some smiling, others seemingly lost in their own thoughts.

After a period of drumming, we place the djembes behind our chairs. Everyone is now more open to share stories, listen, and respect one another. Some share stories of just being tired of being locked up; others talk about yet another continuance; still others speak of bad news from home. Someone who just lost a loved one or a friend murdered on the streets speaks of his anger and frustration at not being out with his family and friends. We listen. The others in the Circle know where he's coming from. They nod their heads in agreement and speak to their feelings when the talking piece comes to them.

The Circles bring us together in a good way according to the values we named and claimed for ourselves. We want to introduce the Circle process as a restorative justice alternative to the otherwise punitive practices currently used in the juvenile justice system. The kids seem to be buying into it. They have told us more than once that they were waiting to come to Circle. It is a place where they can talk about what they are carrying within.

While the drumming Circle is for youth who are being held on adult cases—and some of these youth have been in juvenile detention for better than two years fighting their cases—we gather on a weekly basis for youth who are there for much less time. These kids are being held on juvenile petitions. They will be getting out soon, and we want both to build a relationship with them and to offer them the experience of Circles while they are held. Some stay for longer, but most will be gone within a couple months. Upon their release, they are welcomed and encouraged to join us on the outside in our weekly Circle in the community. The kids, once released, often speak about how hard it is for them to get into school, find a job, or get along with their families at home. They also speak about being jumped or robbed. They share their deep frustrations with a school that treats them as though they were "not good enough."

But our community also has times for celebrating, and we often include Circles as part of our celebrations. Someone graduates from high school or has a birthday. These are times for sharing what these events mean to the young people and their families and friends. At times, we go off to find a place outside the community and gather in Circle and talk about the pressures and stresses of life. These are weekend retreats or times away from life's routine.

For example, we went on a trip to Colorado. It was well prepared (or so we thought) and about eight youth ventured to the mountains. We planned to spend five days and nights climbing to the peak. The rain, the snow, the cooking, and the carrying was more than they could handle. One evening before we reached the peak, the youth called us (adults) into a Circle, and they shared how this was just something that they did not want to continue. While we were disappointed, we heard what they were saying. They were able to speak to us about how they felt.

While we accompany the young people in many aspects of their lives (their jobs, education, counseling, etc), the Circles are how we come together. When we gather in Circle, no matter where we are, we know that it is time to listen to one another. You have to realize that the Circle can change the way you interact with one another.

One last thought: we were asked to give a presentation about our Circle work at the juvenile detention center to a couple of priests from Poland. We were merely going to show them around and talk about our work. In order to do that, we brought down four youth to talk about what it meant to be locked up in the detention center. But before we could get started, the youth said that they needed a Circle. The night before, someone was killed whom two of the youth knew and cared for. So, we went to the closet where we kept our Circle stuff, got out a cloth, a talking piece, a candle, and a few other items, and then we sat in Circle. We shared with one another the pain of losing someone we love. It was powerful; it was more than we could have imagined.

On the way out, the two priests from Poland, said, "That was a most powerful experience." In a real way, the youth taught us a bit about reconciliation.

—Dave Kelly

Father David Kelly founded in 2000 and now directs the Precious Blood Ministry of Reconciliation in St. Michael's parish in Chicago—a community that struggles with issues of poverty, gangs, and racial divisions.

By using Circles, Roca creates that fundamental sense of belonging, building transformational relationships. They love young people whose behavior is not loveable, a wonderful combination of unconditional love and accountability. Then they give them a way and a place where they can manage their behavior and reach their full potential.

Roca epitomizes what the Circle process is all about: a safe, sacred place to learn how to live. Thank you, Carolyn, for your work in sharing Roca with us.

—Sally Wolf
Circle Trainer and Keeper, Executive Director of the Illinois Balanced and Restorative Justice Initiative

The Community Justice for Youth Institute (CJYI) in Chicago, Illinois, is motivated by the core awareness that, no matter where you live, no matter what your circumstances, when children die, everyone is affected. Now more than ever, Chicago needs solutions to end the violence in our communities. Restorative justice provides a way for everyone impacted by violence to be a part of the solution. Our Community Justice for Youth Institute provides training to communities, juvenile justice practitioners, and educators across the city in restorative justice practices, especially peacemaking Circles.

Chicago's restorative justice movement is the story of community leaders connecting to youth on their blocks; of lawyers working in church basements instead of courtrooms; of parents taking more control of how their children are disciplined in school; of educators using peacemaking Circles in their classrooms; and of judges creating space for greater community ownership of young people's futures. Working with youth who are struggling to survive in difficult environments, this movement integrates community and institutional initiatives to change how future generations will deal with conflict.

As nationally recognized experts in restorative justice, CJYI has provided training and technical support to organizations that are doing crucial work in their communities. For example, administrators, educators, and security at Dyett High School on the south side have been trained in the peacemaking Circle process and are now using Circles to diffuse school violence and reintegrate students following suspension and expulsion.

—Cheryl Graves, M.P.H., J.D.

A former clinical law professor, Cheryl has more than ten years of experience conducting restorative justice practices and providing training to communities throughout Chicago and the U.S.

—Margaret Hughes, M.A.

Having worked with girls incarcerated in the Cook County Juvenile Temporary Detention Center, Margaret also has extensive experience training people in the use of community panels for youth and peacemaking Circles.

—Robert Spicer, M.S. ED.

A former teacher, Robert provides training throughout Chicago and Illinois on community engagement and restorative justice practices. He has trained Chicago Public School administrators, teachers, and staff in peacemaking Circles and conducted Circles to resolve conflicts throughout Chicago and the state.

—Ora Schub, J.D.

A former clinical law professor and criminal defense attorney, Ora is known for her work on domestic violence and human rights. She regularly conducts Circle trainings to school systems and youth-related agencies and institutions in the Chicago area.

Much has been written about restorative justice work with juvenile justice systems. However, few, if any, accounts are as compelling as Carolyn Boyes-Watson's description of the application of peacemaking Circle processes in a "youth development" program in a challenging urban setting. Her account is striking in at least two ways.

First, her account of the use of Circle processes in the Roca project in Boston, Massachusetts, is a moving description of how, in a well-formed Circle, participants can actually meet each other in dialogue that calls forth the human desire and capacity for deep empathic connection. In the Roca experience, both the organization as well as those it serves are brought together and transformed in a setting in which the mutual regard and respect—which Circles can cultivate when done well—actually occurs.

Second, the account of what is occurring at Roca is compelling because Boyes-Watson brings the voices of many of the participants into her telling of what is, in reality, a collectively written story. In doing so, she lets these participants speak in their own voices using their ordinary language, rather than the often arcane vocabulary of the academy. At points, someone reading her account can have the distinct sense of being present, as if they were sitting in on what is happening in the Circle practice at Roca.

These two striking features of this important contribution to the growing literature of restorative justice, in general, and Circles, in particular, demonstrates what is possible with sustained, courageous work that is faithful to the deepest assumptions of Circle practice. The first assumption is that everyone wants to be connected in a good way. The second assumption is that, in a safe place constructed by patient Circle work, people who might otherwise not engage each other at the deep level of empathic connection can in fact do so. Out of this experience, people can build a shared future in which all might flourish.

> **—Howard J. Vogel**
> *Professor of Law, Hamline University School of Law,*
> *St. Paul, Minnesota*

Peacemaking Circles and Urban Youth is beautifully written and monumentally helpful in understanding how to use Circles with youth. The book shares openly how the Circle process has shaped Roca's development, providing an excellent resource and vision for us all. This book is a beacon to what is possible and gives a roadmap to Circling.

—Kris Miner
Executive Director of the Saint Croix Valley Restorative Justice Program in Saint Croix, Wisconsin

This is an important book for everyone to read. It provides an inspirational road map on how we need to listen to our youth in respectful and meaningful ways!

—Wanda D. McCaslin
Editor of Justice As Healing: Indigenous Ways *and of the newsletter,* Justice As Healing *from the Native Law Centre, University of Saskatchewan*

My deepest thanks to Carolyn for bringing honor to the Roca Family and providing re-affirmation that Circles work everywhere. Having heard Molly Baldwin speak several times, I was familiar with the extraordinary work being done at Roca, but here it is in one mesmerizing read. Carolyn succeeded in conveying the power of Circle. To borrow a line from a movie, "If you build it, . . . they will come."

This work will resonate with Circle Keepers everywhere and hopefully illuminate the path for all those who work with youth.

—Don Haldeman
Victim Advocate, Graduate Restorative Justice Professor at St. Joseph's University in Philadelphia, Pennsylvania, and Circle keeper

This story of the application of the Circle process and restorative principles to a youth-serving organization provides an excellent example of what you do after you find a talking piece. By adding the Circle process to their best youth development practices, Roca started making community, not just connecting to it. Roca's story has insights for schools, adult-serving agencies, businesses, block clubs, and the faith community. Carolyn tells this story with the eye of a participant: each observation and each anecdote is as fresh as last night's Circle.

—Nancy Riestenberg

Prevention Specialist, Minnesota School Safety Center/ Minnesota Department of Education

About Living Justice Press

A 501(c)(3) tax-exempt, nonprofit publisher on restorative justice

Living Justice Press (LJP) publishes books about social justice and community healing. We focus specifically on restorative justice and peacemaking, and within this field, we concentrate our work in three areas.

First, we publish books that deepen the understanding and use of peacemaking Circles. Circles help people deal with conflicts and harms in ways that promote justice and "being in a good way" as a way of life.

Second, because restorative justice draws directly from Indigenous philosophies and practices, we publish on Indigenous ways of understanding justice. These ways have to do with learning "how to be good relatives"—not only with each other but also with the peoples of the natural world.

Third, we publish the voices of those "in struggle" for justice. Our books seek to apply what we have learned about healing harms between people to the larger and more systemic challenges of addressing harms between Peoples. Through our publishing, we join in working toward justice between Peoples through paths of education, rectifying harms, and transforming our ways of being together.

Peacemaking Circles constitutes our first area of publishing. In fact, we founded Living Justice Press in 2002 precisely to publish *Peacemaking Circles: From Crime to Community* by Kay Pranis, Barry Stuart, and Mark Wedge. Now in its third printing, this book is being used in all sorts of contexts: courts, colleges, tribal courts, tribal colleges, First Nations communities, law schools, universities, churches, law enforcement and probation agencies, prisons, schools, youth centers, juvenile detention facilities, families, and, of course, community justice programs across the country and around the world. The book is even translated into Ukranian.

Peacemaking Circles describes the philosophy and practice of the Circle process—a process that constitutes a major paradigm shift in how we respond to conflicts and harms. One chapter shows how the Circle process can be used in relation with the criminal justice system to create alternatives to incarceration and to support prisoner re-entry. Beyond that specific application, though, the book as a whole has become a core text on the Circle process and how it can be used in many other contexts as well.

Values are an essential part of the Circle process, no matter what the purpose of a particular Circle may be. *Building a Home for the Heart: Using Metaphors in Value-Centered Circles* by Patricia Thalhuber, B.V.M., and Susan Thompson explores ways to use metaphors to promote and deepen this all-important discussion. Drawing on metaphors from the natural world, the book provides concrete examples as well as sample formats for how to use metaphors in Circles. Introducing metaphors inevitably deepens the dialogue about the values we choose to bring to a relationship, situation, or conflict.

The book you now hold in your hands, *Peacemaking Circles and Urban Youth: Bringing Justice Home* by Dr. Carolyn Boyes-Watson, initiates a series of Living Justice Press books that explore how peacemaking Circles can support young people. Since LJP's founding, we have wanted to publish books about how Circles are being used in schools. Across the country, Circles and other restorative practices are becoming a natural part of everyday life for students. This is an exciting and critically important area of restorative justice work. Not only are young people being kept out of the juvenile justice system, but also new generations are being trained in peacemaking values and practices as a way of life.

Another powerful use of Circles with young people focuses on safe driving. Kris Miner, the executive director for the St. Croix Restorative Justice Program, is taking Circles into schools—from kindergarten to college—first to introduce students to the process and then, as they get older, to talk about safety on the road. The largest cause of death for young people is auto accidents. Drinking alcohol and not wearing seat belts are no longer the only causes. Distractions, such as talking on cell phones, text messaging, or talking with passengers, cause many fatal accidents. Funded by The Allstate Foundation, Kris is preparing a manual for driver education instructors and teachers that shares her experiences of using Circles to help youth drive safely and mindfully, and LJP is both honored and delighted to publish it.

Justice As Healing: Indigenous Ways by Wanda D. McCaslin of the Native Law Centre at the University of Saskatchewan focuses on Indigenous approaches to justice. For ten years, the Native Law Centre has published a newsletter called *Justice As Healing*. Selecting from this newsletter, this book gathers a wide range of articles, mostly by Indigenous authors. The authors explore how we can use conflicts to address deep issues in our relationships and communities. They also explore how we can respond to these underlying problems in ways that are healing and transformative for everyone involved. After suffering centuries of invasion, genocide, forced assimilation, and racism, Native communities are rebounding by drawing on their own traditions of community healing and peacemaking. The work carries transformative power, and what these authors share about this process can inspire both Native and non-Native audiences.

LJP's third area of publishing work focuses on applying restorative justice principles and values to working toward justice between Peoples. In general, restorative justice processes begin with hearing the stories on both sides of harm. Through this process, harms are acknowledged, and those who perpetrated and/or benefit from them express genuine remorse and apology for being complicit, knowingly or not, in the suffering of others. On this basis, people work together to make amends, rectify injustices, and do what it takes to "make things right," so that those harmed can become whole again.

In the Footsteps of Our Ancestors: The Dakota Commemorative Marches of the 21st Century, edited by Dakota historian, scholar, and activist Dr. Waziyatawin Angela Wilson, contributes to the first step of this process. Minisota Makoce is the ancestral homeland of the Dakota. This book shares the stories around a long-standing and largely unknown series of horrific harms that happened to the Dakota People in Minnesota. Composed of essays written by participants in the 2002 and 2004 Dakota Commemorative Marches, this book confronts the crimes of colonization, genocide, and forced removal that Euro-Americans inflicted on the Dakota People. It also explores what Dakota people are doing to heal from this history and what White people can do to work for justice today. A *St. Paul Pioneer Press* review stated that the lead article by Dr. Wilson "should be required reading in every school in the state [of Minnesota]." Since this brutal history is not at all unique to Minnesota, the book's call for justice between Peoples is compelling for audiences across the continent.

Waziyatawin is now writing a companion book, *What Does Justice Look Like? The Struggle for Liberation in Dakota Homeland*, designed to initiate public dialogue about what we can do as Peoples to "make things right." Waziyatawin realized the need for this book when she engaged in various discussions about Minnesota's sesquicentennial, which "celebrates" 150 years of statehood. Given the history of genocide for the purpose of stealing land from its Indigenous inhabitants, the book takes up the hard questions: What kind of people celebrates what has been gained through genocide without ever acknowledging the crime? What does the recognition of genocide demand from those in whose name it was waged and who now benefit by possessing the land stolen by these means? What can we do today to "make things right" with the Dakota—most of whom now live in exile in communities scattered across the continent—and with the many Peoples who now occupy the Dakota People's ancestral homeland? These are, indeed, hard questions, but not until we start asking them can we begin the journey to justice.

We at Living Justice Press want to thank you for the time and thought you have given to our publications and for your support in using them in your life and work. We also appreciate your telling your family, friends, colleagues, students, and communities about our books, since that is how books get into the hands of those who want and need them. We invite you to add your name to our mailing list—especially our emailing list—so we can inform you of future books. We are also profoundly grateful for the financial support that more and more of you are giving to LJP to help keep our publishing work going. As we expressed at the beginning of this book, we cannot produce new books or keep existing titles in print without your assistance. We look forward to hearing from you. Finally, we want to thank you for the powerful energies that you give to justice and healing in your own lives and work. You are our inspiration.

Living Justice Press
2093 Juliet Avenue, St. Paul, MN 55105
Tel. (651) 695-1008 • Fax. (651) 695-8564
E-mail: info@livingjusticepress.org
Web site: www.livingjusticepress.org

Terrence M. Moore
Principal
Rise Up Academy

Books from Living Justice Press

On the Circle Process and Its Uses

Peacemaking Circles: From Crime to Community by Kay Pranis, Barry Stuart, and Mark Wedge, ISBN 0-9721886-0-6, paperback, 271 pages, index.

Building a Home for the Heart: Using Metaphors in Value-Centered Circles by Pat Thalhuber, B.V.M., and Susan Thompson, foreword by Kay Pranis, illustrated by Loretta Draths, ISBN 978-0-9721886-3-0, paperback, 224 pages, index.

Peacemaking Circles and Urban Youth: Bringing Justice Home by Carolyn Boyes-Watson, ISBN 978-0-9721886-4-7, paperback, 255 pages (approx.), index.

On Indigenous Justice

Justice As Healing: Indigenous Ways, edited by Wanda D. McCaslin, ISBN 0-9721886-1-4, paperback, 459 pages, index.

On Addressing Harms between Peoples

In the Footsteps of Our Ancestors: The Dakota Commemorative Marches of the 21st Century, edited by Waziyatawin Angela Wilson, ISBN 0-9721886-2-2, oversize paperback, 316 pages, over 100 photographs, color photo insert, index.

What Does Justice Look Like? The Dakota Struggle for Justice in Our Minisota Homeland by Waziyatawin, ISBN 0-9721886-5-7, paperback, 150 pages (approx.), index.

We offer a 20% discount on orders of 10 books or more. We are delighted to receive orders that come directly to us or through our Web site. Our books are also available through amazon.com, and they can be special ordered from most bookstores. Please check our Web site for announcements of new LJP books.

Order by phone, fax, mail, or online at:
2093 Juliet Avenue, St. Paul, MN 55105
Tel. (651) 695-1008 • Fax. (651) 695-8564
E-mail: info@livingjusticepress.org
Web site: www.livingjusticepress.org